HEALTHY
MEDITERRANEAN
COOKING

HEALTHY MEDITERRANEAN COOKING

RENA SALAMAN

PHOTOGRAPHS BY GUS FILGATE

SERIES EDITOR
LEWIS ESSON

FRANCES LINCOLN

To my lovely daughters, Sophie and Alexandra

Frances Lincoln Limited
4 Torriano Mews, Torriano Avenue
London NW5 2RZ

First Frances Lincoln paperback edition 1999

British Library Cataloguing in Publication Data
A catalogue record for this book is available from the British Library

ISBN 0 7112 1403 4

Printed in China

3 5 7 9 10 8 6 4

NOTES
Throughout the book both metric and imperial quantities are given. Use either all metric or all imperial, as the two are not necessarily interchangeable.

Nutritional Information
The figures given in the nutritional information panel that accompanies each recipe are per serving and have been rounded off to the nearest whole number. Optional ingredients and variations have not been included in the calculations and the figures are based on the largest number of suggested servings.

The ranges given for fat, protein and carbohydrate content are based on the proportion each makes of the total calorie content as follows.

Total fat: Low = under 20%; Medium = 20-33%; High = over 33%
Saturated fat: Low = under 5%; Medium = 5-10%; High = over 10%
Protein: Low = under 15%; Medium = 15-20%; High = over 20%
Carbohydrate: Low = under 50%; Medium = 50-60%; High = over 60%

Please note that such a system can occasionally produce results that seem surprising when not viewed in a wider context. For example, a salad dressed with only 2 tablespoons of oil can have a very low overall calorie count, so its fat content then reads as 'high' in this system. However, were that salad to be analysed together with just one accompanying slice of bread the increase in total calories could reduce the level of fat to 'medium' or even 'low'.

Throughout the book the olive oil content of dishes has been reduced from traditional generous amounts and, if you are attempting to curb fat intake, you may lower them even further. However, its use has been kept at an optimum level to achieve authentic flavours and to ensure the benefits of olive oil's health-giving properties when consumed in moderation.

CONTENTS

A MEDITERRANEAN JOURNEY

Romantics and simple travellers alike have eulogized the Mediterranean through the centuries. Shelley in his 'Ode to the West Wind' sang about its blue waters, Goethe spoke of 'the land where the lemon trees blossom' and Norman Douglas in *Siren Land* urged his readers to 'mediterraneanize' themselves, even if only for a season.

As I sit under the shade of the big glossy-leaved mulberry tree in our garden on an Aegean island and gaze at the blue expanse beyond the hills where the sea quietly joins the horizon, I feel the full impact of all those other travellers. There it all is... The lemon trees (admittedly not flowering, as it is late July), the almond trees loaded with heavy fruit, the fig trees with their erotic smell under the midday sun, and of course the queen of all – the olive tree. Could we perceive the Mediterranean without the olive tree?

Then the different characters start to parade as if out of a play. First morning visitor is Stavros, who collects the rubbish with his mule during the summer, and who is passionate about and an expert on trees. He sips his tiny Greek coffee and gives an appraisal of our trees. The mulberry will have to be pruned severely if we are to limit its production of huge white sugary fruit that attracts the wasps in thousands earlier in July. (I would have risked my life sitting under it two weeks ago.) The vines will need some manure if the grapes are to be improved, and the almond trees are getting straggly.

On another note, did we hear about the extraordinary amounts of squid that Nikos the carpenter caught last night? Yes, we later did as a bag full of wonderful squid arrived as a present from Nikos, distributing his excessive catch after complaints from his wife that she has run out of space in the fridge.

Stavros's wife Nina runs the family *taverna* in one of the cobbled streets at the heart of the village. Stavros mentions that our favourite *yiouvetsi* – a dish of goat or lamb and pasta with fresh tomatoes and quantities of garlic – is on the menu tonight as Tassos the shepherd has slaughtered a couple of his goats. How could we miss that? Tassos's goats roam the hills around the village, as their bells announce them daily, and they feed on the purple flowers of the thyme that covers the hillsides. Sometimes they also feed on people's plants over the garden walls and then they are not popular at all. As for Nina's intimacy with a first-class *yiouvetsi*, we are well aware of that.

Next the tiny, bird-like but agile, Penelope – her woollen socks drooping round her ankles and her ruby-studded black patent leather shoes, a couple of sizes too large for her tiny feet – almost hops over the garden wall, with her apron gathered. Some fresh eggs from her hens are nestling in there. They will make a perfect omelette, cooked with some sweet tomatoes at lunch time.

And then arrives old bony one-toothed Barba Nikos with his hawk-like nose and a leathered skin like a lizard's, who builds the lace-like stone walls around our gardens. He brings golden apricots from his trees and bunches of *rigani* – oregano – and gives us the latest village gossip while sipping a cold beer. He recounts his early morning outing with his friend from Athens, Stratigous, 'the General', in search of *pikrohorto*, a frightfully bitter herb which, when taken as a tisane, lowers the blood pressure and makes you immortal like the gods, according to Nikos. Having tried it a few years ago, I can still feel my teeth numb

with the excessive bitterness. Can this have been the way Socrates felt as he drank his *conium*, I wondered.

These are the different puzzle pieces that constitute the Mediterranean. The people, the distinctive trees, the aromatic hillsides, the sea – with all its bounty – and the delicious food that has been born out of the combinations of all these. Following the food trail around the Mediterranean is like following the people. Although each country has its distinctive signature in the kitchen, the same primary ingredients play first violin and so a number of similar dishes is to be found around this fabled sea. The seasonal vegetables quickly fried or grilled and served with fresh soured or grilled cheeses or garlicky sauces, or occasionally pulped into savoury dips, the fish and the seafood, the salads which appear in unusual combinations with fruit and nuts and the winter soups made with beans, chickpeas and lentils.

There are also those unmistakable underlying links which are olive oil and the herbs that enhance the dishes. It is not only the dishes themselves, however, but also the way they are served and the spirit in which they are consumed, as life revolves and evolves round the table in the Mediterranean.

Finally, to the poets and travellers past and present eulogizing about the Mediterranean, most recently doctors and dieticians have added their voices – this time about the Mediterranean diet and not any more just about its tastes and colours, but about its healthiness. The grains, pulses, fresh fruit and vegetables, the high-protein fish, lean meat and poultry, the olive oil and wine that are its staples are now recognized as providing the ultimate healthy diet. Low in cholesterol and saturated fats and high in fibre and vitamins, it also supplies an abundance of the protective agents that are thought actively to combat disease and enhance life expectancy.

THE HEALTHY MEDITERRANEAN DIET

What exactly is this healthy Mediterranean diet? To me, this diet recently appraised as healthy is simply what I was brought up on – the seasonal vegetables cooked with lots of garlic and onions and brought alive with lemons or tomatoes, the bean and lentil soups in the winter, the cheese pies, the abundant fruit, and fresh salads with every meal. This was what we and our friends and neighbours ate daily, and we did not seem to have weight problems, cardiovascular disorders or too many other ailments.

Of course the main protagonist of the cooking pot, as well as the table, is the aromatic fruity green olive oil which, among fats, is the richest source of the desirable monounsaturated fatty acids contained in its large amounts of oleic acid (see page 10).

The original research project on the subject was carried out by the United Nations on Crete in the 1950s, prompted by the history of longevity on the island, as well as the absence of cardiovascular disease. However, we knew nothing of this research or its convincing results. Olive oil was simply at the root of our lives. We did not know butter, as it virtually did not exist – even now I hardly use it and I don't miss it. As for meat, it was served in small quantities on Sundays and then more often as minced meat in stuffed vegetables or in meat rissoles.

Instead, we had fish and seafood of all kinds. Everyone knew that fish was lean and healthy, containing a number of nutrients and vitamins. Our grandmothers had a standard phrase for seafood: 'Good for the eyes [containing phosphorus], the blood [it lowers cholesterol] and the brain [vitamin E]'. Modern research has proved that it is the omega-3 fatty acids contained in fish oil that have all these beneficial qualities. So, squid, cuttlefish, mussels and occasionally razor clams were made into *pilaffs* or fried to accompany the lentil soups or bean salads. Slim elongated silver anchovies sprinkled with garlic, fresh tomatoes and olive oil or small whole tuna dotted with garlic and wrapped in paper were sent to the ovens at the local bakers. Fish soups were assembled with a variety of different small bony fish called *petropsara* – rockfish – and the occasional eel. Salt cod was treated in a multitude of ways and a small piece of it would go a long way. The diet was a combination of frugality and tradition. The latter being itself born out of frugality anyway.

The abundance of vegetables and pulses – with their many nutrients, their vitamins, minerals and fibre – made up the main character of the Mediterranean diet. And olive oil was, on the whole, what gave flavour to the dishes. Admittedly it was quite often used in rather large quantities. However olive oil, as we have seen, has been proved beneficial to health. So the Mediterranean diet is healthy in its very nature. With a few adjustments it can become even more so.

Writing this book has been a rather natural outcome of all this. Nevertheless, in an effort to make the recipes even healthier, if that is possible, I have reduced the amounts of olive oil used – although not too drastically, so its flavour is still prevalent. If you are counting calories you can lower the amount of olive oil (and nuts) even further.

Throughout the book, however, the focus is on vegetables, pulses and seafood. Butter and cream have been kept to a minimum and they can be omitted altogether. Cheese, particularly in Italian cooking, is so indispensable that it would have seemed unnatural to eliminate it altogether. Anyway, cheeses like Parmesan have such a powerful flavour that only very little is needed. There are, however, other important factors in the Mediterranean diet's healthy character; that is, how a meal is assembled and consumed.

MEDITERRANEAN MEALS

The Mediterranean *mezze* approach to a meal concentrates on variety. I prefer it not only because of its appeal to the palate but also because of its lighter character. It also inevitably slows the meal down, which is a good thing in itself.

For instance, for a fairly lavish meal with friends I serve two or three small courses, some cold and others hot, one after the other so that their flavours can be fully experienced. These may be Melitzanosalata (page 43), Tyropitakia (page 49) and Tabbouleh (page 145) or Roast Courgettes with Salsa Verde (page 44) and Puy Lentils with Dill, Salsa Verde and Roast Peppers (page 128). Then we may have a salad and after that have a main course in the form of an Asparagus Risotto (page 72) or fish, for instance. The *mezze* obviously can be as varied and elaborate as the situation dictates, or it can be simple and frugal.

For our family meals at home in Athens we would always have a large crusty loaf of fresh bread on the table. Additionally, there were bowls of olives and plates of greenery, such as rocket and little radishes or spring onions and cucumbers. People would help themselves to all these throughout the meal. By stopping and introducing a new flavour, people slow down, which is healthy in itself, but also the total quantity consumed diminishes. So not only the meal itself was healthy, but so was the way it was eaten.

When planning a meal, try to add variety. Try to make the combinations well-balanced and interesting. Invite some friends and try cooking some of the dishes in this book, serving them in the Mediterranean fashion with a good local wine. Then just sit back and observe the results. At least liveliness – if not intoxication – will be hovering in the air.

Rena Salaman, Summer 1995

SOME MEDITERRANEAN INGREDIENTS

'Let food be your medicine' said the father of medicine, Hippocrates (460-337 BC).

OLIVE OIL AND OLIVES

If there was one tree with which to identify the Mediterranean, it would be the olive tree, *Olea europaea*, which has grown wild in the area since time immemorial. I have seen wild gnarled olive trees being grafted and have experienced their miraculous conversion once they start to sprout tame branches with bigger leaves. Weather-beaten, water-starved and scorched by the strong summer sun, they still manage to produce their wondrous fruit.

The olive tree, with its beautiful silver leaves, has been the source of the most important ingredient in the Mediterranean kitchen, olive oil, and another important ingredient on the table, the olive itself. According to historical sources, both of these were used abundantly in ancient Greece and it was the ancient seafaring Greeks who brought the olive tree west as far as Spain and Provence.

Fresh olives off the tree are inedible as they are incredibly bitter. Take a tiny bite off one and your mouth will be completely numb. So it is a marvel that this inedible fruit can be transformed in such a way by the time it reaches the table. This is done by cracking or slicing the olives and immersing them in cold water, which has to be changed daily for at least ten to fifteen days. Once through this process, they lose their bitterness and they can then be salted and flavoured with added aromatics and spices.

When the olives are picked from the tree while still unripe and green, which happens in early September, they are treated for their bitterness and they are then our familiar green olives, which have a refreshing taste and harder texture. Once the olives have turned dark violet-blue or black on the tree – which starts to happen around the middle of October – then these black olives have a more complex flavour than the green ones. However, black olives can be tricky, as I have found by experience. Occasionally, after we have soaked them in water to extract their bitterness they can become completely tasteless and bland. It is at that stage that we marinate them with salt, garlic cloves, bay leaves, coriander seeds, chillies and anything else that takes our fancy.

Olives ripen earlier or later according to the position of the trees, the soil and the weather. For the purposes of olive oil, they have to be picked at a medium stage, when they are still hard and on the tree, before they shrivel and fall off. Green unripe olives produce a small yield of olive oil, which also contains a lower quantity of oleic acid. As the olives ripen they produce more oil, with a higher yield of oleic acid. Oleic acid is the principal factor that determines their classification. 'Extra-virgin' oil must contain less than 1% oleic acid, in fact, the cognoscenti believe that it should not be more than 0.5%. Olive oil with a higher acidity of anything between 1.5% and 3% is generally classified as 'virgin'. Extra-virgin olive oil must also meet high standards of flavour, aroma and colour.

The production of high-quality olive oil is very labour-intensive. The olives must be picked by hand, as any mechanical process might bruise them. Once harvested, they have to be transported to the olive mill as soon as possible before they start to ferment as their acidity level increases. There they are washed mechanically in cold water and the leaves and small branches are separated from the fruit. The olives are

then crushed and mixed with water. The oil, once separated from the water in a centrifuge, drips into vats. Generally today any oil from this first mechanical pressing (as opposed to later chemical extraction) is claimed to be from the 'first cold pressing' (a term not defined by any international agreement), so one must not pay too much heed to such a description on the bottle. The main factors in flavour are olive variety and local soil and climate.

Olive oil has a great diversity in taste. It can be golden, sweet and smooth – as is French olive oil often – or dark green with a strong fruity taste like Greek olive oil. This is a matter of personal choice and it frequently means that one can use different oils for different occasions and dishes. Throughout this book I have not specified extra-virgin oil in the recipes because I assume that one would not want to use anything else.

Olive oil does not keep for ever and it has to be stored in a dark and cool place. In my experience on Alonnisos, where the oil is stored in large *pytharia,* it

holds its taste for about two years, and after that it may go rancid, developing an unmistakable and unpleasant 'engine oil' taste and smell.

Recently a lot has been written about olive oil and its beneficial effects on our health. Basically olive oil contains no cholesterol and it is a monounsaturated fat, which contains a large concentration of Vitamin E and HDLs (High Density Lipoproteins). HDLs lower cholesterol in the system and also act against the harmful LDLs (low-density lipoproteins), which in turn accumulate cholesterol and deposit it on the arterial walls. Olive oil not only contains these valuable HDLs but also – unlike other oils – it does not destroy the body's own natural resources of these HDLs. Polyunsaturated oils like the vegetable oils, on the other hand, while they lower the harmful LDLs also deplete the body's own beneficial HDLs.

VEGETABLES

Vegetables are a natural source of all kinds of nutrients, such as proteins as well as vitamins, minerals, fibre and antioxidants, these last being vigorous anti-cancer agents.

ARTICHOKES

The globe artichoke is for me the queen of vegetables. It can be eaten raw, when its heart is sliced thinly into salads, or cooked in casseroles or omelettes or stuffed. Artichokes also signify spring, as they start to appear in the markets in March. Historically the artichoke, which is a cultivated variety of the cardoon, was developed in fifteenth-century Italy and soon spread to Greece and the other countries around the Mediterranean.

Before use, the inedible hairy choke lying just above the heart needs to be removed. However, very young artichokes sometimes have little or no developed choke and may be cooked and eaten whole. The artichoke discolours readily, so needs to be immersed in acidulated water or brushed with lemon juice after preparation. Artichokes are a good source of Vitamin A, folate, potassium and calcium.

AUBERGINES

Although seemingly a quintessential Mediterranean vegetable, the aubergine actually came from the East, probably India. Botanically it belongs to the Solanaceae family, like the tomato, pepper and potato.

It originally tended to be bitter, so it was imperative once sliced either to immerse it in salted water for half an hour or to sprinkle the slices with salt and then rinse them. Nowadays, with modern varieties, I find there is no bitterness, so it is not necessary to go through this procedure any more – not with Mediterranean varieties anyway. I know that in places like India and Ceylon some aubergines can still be bitter, so beware.

It is in Turkey that the love of aubergines is proverbial and they will be found there in a plethora of dishes. Aubergines are a good source of calcium, vitamin A and a smaller amount of vitamin C.

GARLIC

One wonders how Mediterranean food would have developed without the presence of garlic. This is one of the oldest and greatest flavouring ingredients, as well as being much used as a medicine and in pagan rituals. It has been worshipped as a god and its strong aroma has been associated with the devil. Its original habitat may have been Western Asia and botanists believe that it came to Mesopotamia and Egypt via Asia Minor.

Garlic is rich in vitamins B and C, and in phosphorus, potassium and calcium, as well as in the

antioxidant mineral selenium. It helps sugar metabolize, so it is used in the treatment of both diabetes and hypoglycaemia. It aids digestion and its content of allicin, which invades the proteins in germs and destroys them, makes it also antibacterial. It also has anti-inflammatory qualities and is thus good against arthritis. Nowadays, it is believed to lower cholesterol and to purify the blood.

The taste of garlic varies according to its age. When it is young, with firm and juicy creamy-white cloves, it has quite a sweet taste; when it has been sitting around for a while, feels soft and papery and the cloves are a dull, yellow colour and look shrivelled, it has a somewhat acrid taste and is to be avoided. In the spring, fresh new season's garlic can be bought. Thin and elegant, this resembles spring onions and its taste is delicately fresh but unmistakable. Thinly sliced it makes a lovely addition to salads.

The best way to crush garlic is to peel it, sprinkle a little salt over it and rest the blade of a knife on it, then press with the heel of the hand to crush it and release its essential oils.

OKRA

Okra, also known descriptively as 'ladies' fingers', are the green pods of a tall annual, *Abelmoschus esculentus*, which can reach a height of 2 metres / 6 ft. The plant's green pods are covered with a light prickly skin, so the okra pickers have to wear gloves to protect their fingers against skin irritations. The pods can vary in size enormously, according to the variety. They have to be handled gently so that they do not get bruised or, worse, squashed, as this will allow their mucilaginous juices to pour out.

Okra, which originates from Africa, has a sweet taste and a pleasurable melting texture. To prepare it you have to pare the conical head lightly with a slanting movement and then trim off the black tip at the other end very slightly. (To simplify matters you can just cut the top horizontally, but be careful not to cut too deep.)

Okra is mostly used whole and intact in the Mediterranean, but there may be instances where it is first sliced to allow its mucilaginous substances to be incorporated in the dish, for instance in the classic New Orleans gumbo.

Okra contains a good amount of vitamin A and a smaller amount of vitamin C.

PEPPERS

Both sweet peppers (*Capsicum annuum*) and chillies (*C. frutescens*) are members of the Solanaceae or nightshade family, which also includes tomatoes and potatoes. Like them, they came from the New World with Columbus in the fifteenth century. A year after his first voyage, the first seeds of *C. annuum* arrived in Spain. It was there that it established itself and got into the kitchens either roasted whole, or dried and pounded into a powder to be used instead of the black pepper which had come from India. This ground red pepper was paprika, although it did not then have the name, but instead was called West Indian pepper. This was not only a flavouring, but it also added brilliant colour to sauces.

There is a bewildering array of different varieties of capsicums, probably over three hundred, with a multitude of shapes, sizes and colours. These extend from the sweet bell peppers to mildly pungent and hot ones, such as the ancho, serrano, jalapeño, poblano and the fiery hot habanero from the West Indies. Peppers, particularly red ones, are an invaluable source of vitamins C and A. Red peppers also contain an enormous amount of beta-carotene, a valuable antioxidant.

Paprika

This red powder, made from a ground dried variety of sweet pepper, is lightly sweet at first but has a slightly bitter aftertaste. It is used mostly in the cooking of Spain, Hungary and North Africa.

Pimentón

From the word *pimiento*, the Spanish for pepper, in the Spanish kitchen pimentón is the most popular seasoning after salt. It is a red powder, similar to paprika, made from dried peppers (mostly the Ñora variety) or

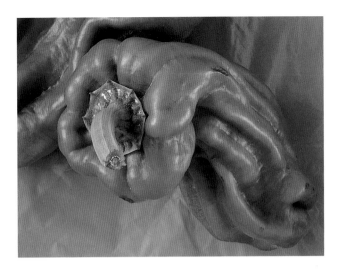

sometimes, as in Extremadura, oak-smoked peppers, and it can be either sweet – *dulce* – or pungent, which could mean hot or sour-sweet – *picante* – according to the variety of peppers from which it is made.

Antep Pepper

A common ingredient around Turkey, its brilliant red colour seems always to put a presence at the table. It is made from a long red, slightly hot pepper which is dried and then flaked and originates from Gaziantep, in South-East Turkey – hence its name.

Urfa Pepper

Flakes of dried pepper, like the antep, but with a darker, purple hue. This is because the pepper is lightly toasted, which also gives it a slight sourness. In Turkey urfa pepper is traditionally served with kebabs and raw onions.

PURSLANE

Purslane, with its larger silvery-coloured furry leaves and thick fleshy, cacti-like stems, has a light lemony, refreshing taste and the wild variety in particular makes an unusual and refreshing salad. It should be trimmed of the thick stems at the bottom, then leaves and stems chopped coarsely and dressed with an aromatic olive oil and lemon juice. It can also be combined with diced cucumber or with other greens. Its most notable presence is in Fattoush (page 138).

ROCKET

The bright green serrated leaves of rocket, with their strong almost spicy taste and peppery finish, are indispensable in a mixed salad. They are loved all over the Mediterranean, particularly in Italy (the Italians' beloved *arugula*) in Greece (*roka*) and in Turkey. Rocket grows like a weed, but it quickly goes to seed and the leaves should be picked young.

Traditionally it was harvested growing wild like dandelions. The younger leaves have a milder taste and a lovely texture and can be made into a salad by themselves, perhaps with shavings of Parmesan on top as served in Italy. Alternatively, when they are older and stronger-tasting, they are better mixed with other salad greens and lettuces, including radicchio. Young leaves can be used whole, but older and coarser leaves are best first trimmed of thick stems.

The sharply appetising taste of rocket goes well with cheese, fish and even fruit. The leaves are packed with vitamins C and B and folate.

SWISS CHARD

Chard belongs to the same family as beetroot, sugar beet and spinach. The leaves, which have a sweet and meadowy taste, are perfect for wrapping food. As the ribbed stems of chard can be quite hard, for most purposes it is best to trim them off. They are very tasty on their own, but need longer cooking. Like spinach, chard contains vitamin C, carotene, iron, potassium and folic acid. Chard is also a very good source of fibre.

TOMATOES

It is quite a paradox that the brilliantly scarlet tomato, which is instantly associated with the Mediterranean and is indispensable to its cooking, is not a local inhabitant but an immigrant. It was brought to Spain from the Americas by Christopher Columbus in the sixteenth century, but did not become generally popular until much later. Its name is derived from the Aztec word *tomatl,* although it was originally known in Spain as *pomo d'oro* – golden apple – as the original varieties seen there were a brilliant yellow in colour.

Tomatoes are low in calories, and contain a large amount of vitamin A as well as vitamins C and E, and minerals such as calcium, potassium, iron and phosphorus. They are also rich in beta-carotene, possibly the most effective antioxidant, and levels of this increase when tomatoes are grilled or roasted.

Preserved Tomatoes, Tomato Paste and Sun-dried Tomatoes

It was the task of my grandmother, along with the other matriarchs of our neighbouring households, to preserve tomatoes in different forms at the end of each summer. First, the small plum tomatoes would be preserved whole in jars, not unlike today's familiar tins of tomatoes. However, the real task – and one that was done on a rather large scale – was making and preserving tomato paste.

Ordinary unevenly shaped large tomatoes were cut in half and sprinkled with salt. They were then exposed to the strong summer sun for two to three days, until shrivelled. They were then boiled down with more salt and finally the thick pulp was pressed through a sieve. This was stored in jars for use throughout the winter, the top of each sealed with a layer of olive oil.

For the majority of us, however, the colourful parade of tins, jars and packets of tomatoes in the shops – whole, chopped or liquidized (when it is called passata), or the jars and tubes of tomato paste, have eliminated this task. Sun-dried tomatoes are a recent addition and originated in Italy. As described above, these tomatoes have been sliced in two, sprinkled with salt and exposed to the hot summer sun until completely dried up. Nowadays in the south of Italy, particularly in Puglia, where quantities of sun-dried tomatoes are produced, the drying is often actually done in slow ovens.

Sun-dried tomatoes have a unique taste, with their concentrated sunny flavours, and they can be used to enhance a number of dishes such as pasta, salads, stuffings, and so on. They can be bought dry, in which case they have to be reconstituted in warm water before they are used, or they come preserved in oil and ready to use.

VINE LEAVES

In Greece, as well as the Middle East, vine leaves are used to wrap and cook food. Stuffings made with rice, onions, herbs and nuts and with or without meat make delicious Dolmathes (see pages 126-7). Vine leaves are also used to wrap fish before either baking or grilling, when they impart their aroma and lemony flavour to the dish. They are traditionally used young and fresh at the beginning of the summer. Alternatively, they can be bought preserved in brine from Greek shops. These tend to be very salty and should be rinsed carefully first.

If you have access to fresh vine leaves you can freeze them. Rinse them first, dip them briefly in a bowl of boiling water and drain them. Pile them in groups of twenty-five, roll them up and place them in a freezer-proof container. Allow them to defrost completely for two to three hours before using them. Vine leaves contain some vitamins and a large amount of carotene and are a good source of fibre.

PULSES

BEANS

Beans are a staple in the Mediterranean, although not indigenous as most varieties are visitors from the New World. They come in different colours, sizes and shapes. Some countries seem to favour some more than others. The most popular and commonly used is the white elongated cannellini bean. Italy, however, has a preference for the marbled red-and-white-skinned borlotti bean. France treasures the smaller white haricot bean. They are used in soups, in purées, in casseroles with meat and sausages and in salads.

As well as the lengthy soaking required for all pulses, most types of bean need to be boiled rapidly for a few minutes and the water then discarded before further cooking to remove toxins and make them more digestible. Beans are an excellent source of protein, calcium, iron, sodium and vitamin A.

Dried Broad Beans

These can be bought whole or skinned and flaked. They are the hardest to cook among pulses, particularly when whole with skins on. In either case they definitely have to be soaked overnight. When they are used for dishes such as the Egyptian Tamia, Lebanese Falafel or the Moroccan Byesar (page 42) you need to buy the skinned variety.

CHICKPEAS

A native of the Mediterranean, they were served in ancient Greece, both as a staple and as a dessert, for which purpose they were roasted. Their nutty taste makes wonderful casseroles, soups and velvety thick dips of all kinds like the Middle Eastern Hummus (page 40). They also make excellent combinations with green vegetables, such as spinach and chard. It is perhaps in Spain, where they are called *garbanzos*, that they have been used most imaginatively. Chickpeas contain vitamin B, potassium and iron.

LENTILS

Natives of the Mediterranean, lentils come in different sizes and colours. They can be grey-green, brown, or slate-colour and they can be large or small. I find the small green or grey-green varieties have the best flavours. French Puy lentils, which are one of these types, are wonderful. There are also the small Egyptian lentils, which have an orange colour once skinned. Lentils have a nutty taste and they are a good source of protein, calcium, iron, selenium and vitamin A.

FRUIT

'Outside the yard is a big orchard on both sides of the gates, of four acres, and a hedge runs along each side of it, and there tall leafy trees have grown, pears and pomegranates and shiny fruited apples and sweet figs and leafy olives; and their fruit never fails winter or summer ... pear upon pear grows old and apple upon apple, grapes upon grapes and fig upon fig.' (Homer's *Odyssey* 7. 112-21.)

Fruit makes an astounding source of fibre and nutrients, and occasionally even more so in its dried form, like figs, apricots and raisins or currants. Fresh fruit is also very low in calories.

FIGS

Fig trees probably originated in Asia Minor, but they grow wild all over the Mediterranean as they are quite hardy with strong roots. They can survive the dry and hot summer months without need of watering and still produce their sugary fruit.

In ancient Greece the fig tree and its fruit had erotic connotations and played a strong part in folklore. With its strong smell, the tree is apparently a powerful hallucinatory source, and in Greek folklore people are not supposed to sleep under it as they may go mad. Figs were served in ancient Greece as an appetizer. Athenaeos quotes the poet Lynceus of Samos who mentions the local custom of eating figs with the appetizers rather than among the desserts. He was my inspiration for the dish of figs with Mozzarella cheese on page 46. Figs contain calcium, potassium and iron.

GRAPES

Grapes have grown wild around the eastern Mediterranean and the fruit – as well as wine made from it – has been enjoyed since antiquity. Red grapes have a high content of an antioxidant called quercetin and their skins contain a natural pesticide which when taken into the system prevents thrombosis and boosts the generation of the cholesterol-lowering high-density lipoproteins (HDLs). Dried grapes – raisins – are particularly rich sources of potassium and iron.

LEMONS

The lemon probably originated in South-east Asia, like all citrus fruits, and Tom Stobart says in his *Herbs, Spices and Flavourings* that it had reached Greece and Italy by the end of the third century BC. Lemon juice is an important souring agent, but it is its zest which has the wonderful aromatic oil. The zest should be finely grated or peeled and chopped finely before use. Lemons are rich in vitamin C and they also contain a good amount of folic acid.

Most lemons on sale nowadays have been coated in a wax containing fungicidal chemicals which prolong the life of the fruit. This is obviously advantageous for the fruit trade, but not necessarily for the human body. So, when planning to use lemon zest in a dish, it makes sense to look out for unwaxed fruit.

Preserved Lemons

Pickled lemons are indispensable in Moroccan cooking, particularly for their *tajines*. They are also very refreshing chopped finely into salads. One sees monumental glass jars filled with them in the *soukhs*. They are easy to pickle in brine at home, in a process not very different from that used to pickle olives.

LIMES

The small, bushy and thorny lime tree, like other citrus fruit trees, originated in South-east Asia. Its fruits are round and smaller than lemons, and of a vivid green colour. What distinguishes them from lemons is their strong aroma and taste, which is quite sour compared to that of a lemon. Its fragrant zest sprinkled over dishes adds a tropical note.

Dried Limes

These are mainly used in the Gulf countries and in Iran. The best ones are those that have been left to dry on the tree. For commercial reasons, however, limes are nowadays mostly dried artificially, which results in an inferior flavour. Even so, they add a wonderful sour taste to vegetables and meat stews.

POMEGRANATES

The pomegranate certainly wins the beauty contest among fruits. I cannot think of anything more stunning than the sparkling regal vermilion colour of the curvy pomegranate with its frilly crown. The pomegranate came from Persia, where it was cultivated four thousand years ago.

Patience is required to extract the seeds from the skin and the bitter yellow pith. It is best to extract them to a plate and then eat them with a spoon. They are wonderful sprinkled into salads, fruit salads and all kinds of cooked dishes. Pomegranates contain a respectable amount of vitamin C.

Pomegranate Syrup

The juice of pomegranates has been used as a souring agent for centuries. It can either be used fresh or boiled to a paste – not to be confused with sweet syrupy Grenadine (also made from pomegranates) – for use throughout the year. It is very popular all over the Middle East, particularly in the Lebanon and Turkey where it is used for salad dressings and in dips or in vegetable casseroles. Its sweet-and-sour taste adds a new dimension to any dish.

GRAINS

BULGAR

Bulgar (also bulghur or burghul), or 'cracked wheat' originated in Mesopotamia. References to it can be found in the Bible but also in some ninth-century BC Assyrian tablets, where one of the dishes mentioned is *kubba* (in Iraq) or *kibbe* (in Syria), made with cracked wheat and stuffed with meat and spices. It was also used by the ancient Greeks as *khondros*. It was the most common grain in the Middle East before the advent of imported and expensive rice.

Traditionally in the Middle East, bulgar is made by

dropping wheat grains into boiling water and cooking them until almost soft. They are then drained and spread on terraces and left for three days, being stirred twice daily. The grain dries and becomes wrinkled in the heat. It is then shelled and spread in the sun again, which separates the dried husks and gives the grain a nutty taste. It is then ground coarsely. This explains how little cooking it requires.

Bulgar has been widely used in the Middle East in pilaffs, in stuffings for vegetables or vine leaves, in soups, mixed with meat and made into kebabs, and in salads such as the Lebanese Tabbouleh (see page 145).

Couscous

Couscous is a tiny round soft pale-yellow grain made from durum wheat flour which constitutes the Moroccan, Tunisian and Algerian national dish. In all these countries, couscous is served with combinations of meat, poultry or fish with vegetables, spices, herbs – and perhaps dried fruit and nuts.

Most of the couscous sold nowadays has been pre-cooked, so all one has to do is to reconstitute the grain in an amount of water (or stock) equal to its volume for fifteen to twenty minutes. Once the liquid has been absorbed, run your fingers through the grain, lifting it in the air and letting the grains tumble down to separate them and break up any lumps.

Apart from its use as the traditional accompaniment to meat, poultry or fish tajines in North Africa, couscous makes the basis for wonderful salads combined with fruit, fresh herbs and other ingredients, as in the Couscous and Peach Salad on page 83, or it can be used for stuffings.

Polenta

Polenta is the speciality of Northern Italy and particularly Venice, Lombardy and Piedmont. It never conquered the South, where pasta has remained the reigning monarch. Modern polenta – *puls* in Latin – is a mixture of corn meal and water. According to Anna Del Conte in her fascinating *Secrets from an Italian Kitchen*, polenta was originally made from a variety of cereals and during the Renaissance barley, chestnuts, broad beans and millet flour were used.

Corn, along with tomatoes, beans and peppers, came to Europe from the New World later, with Columbus. The yellow grain arrived from Spain in the Rialto market in Venice, where it was immediately christened *granoturco* – Turkish grain – for no sensible explanation other than its exotic colour and its distinct foreignness. By the sixteenth century, with the decline and fall of the Eastern Empire, Venetians and the peasants of the mainland were quite poor, so this easy-to-grow crop was to become a staple around the Po Valley, where it was first cultivated. And so yellow polenta had arrived in Venice.

As a staple for the poor it was mostly eaten by itself or sometimes with milk or butter. Leftovers were grilled and eaten for breakfast the next day or for lunch, when it was adorned with cheap accompaniments, such as beans, onions, lard or crackling and for those who could afford it *baccalà* – salt cod. This was *cucina povera* in all its inventiveness.

Polenta makes an ideal background for juxtaposing bold flavours. Its versatility lies in its constantly changing character: with melted cheese such as Fontina or Gorgonzola added in at the final moments of its cooking it becomes rich and sumptuous; with a rich stew, such as the Venetian classic *polenta con seppie nere* (polenta with cuttlefish in their own ink or squid, as on page 78), it becomes dynamic.

HERBS & SPICES

BASIL *Ocimum basilicum*

Basil may have come to Europe from India via the Middle East, Tom Stobart says in his book *Herbs, Spices and Flavourings*. It has holy associations, and in Greece small bunches of the herb are used in the church to sprinkle holy water around and also often to adorn icons.

Basil is probably the most important herb in the kitchen and it is the Italians who have used it most. In Genoese Pesto (page 33), the basil-based sauce for pasta, it comes into its own. It also has a wonderful affinity with tomatoes. Its sweet aroma is unparalleled and it can transform a simple tomato sauce into an exotic delicacy. It is best to tear basil by hand rather than chopping it with a knife, as this bruises it.

CORIANDER *Coriandrum sativum*

Coriander is indigenous to the Mediterranean area. It had been used by Hippocrates medicinally in ancient Greece, and seeds of it were found in the Franhthi cave in Argolis which dates them at about 7000 BC. Both its fresh leaves and its small round brown-coloured seeds, with their warm aroma, are used in cooking, particularly in the Middle East and North Africa. The seeds are used whole or ground in both savoury and sweet dishes as well as for pickling.

CUMIN *Cuminum cyminum*

In the Mediterranean, cumin is among the most popular of spices. Its presence is made unmistakable by its powerful aroma. I regard cumin as a cool spice with an elegant taste. It originated in Egypt and the

Middle East and then spread eastwards and westwards. Its light coloured green-grey seeds can be used either whole or ground, but they always taste richer when they have been roasted first.

MARJORAM AND OREGANO *Origanum majorana; O. vulgare*
Native to the Mediterranean, these small woody plants, with tiny leaves and small white flowers, grow wild on the hillsides and in disused fields. Known in Greece as *rigani*, oregano is loved by all and it is indispensable in the kitchen. It is a favourite in everything from roasts and kebabs to pizzas, casseroles and marinades. This is the herb that I could not cook without. Even in the depths of winter its aroma can instantly transport me to a Greek hillside.

PARSLEY *Petroselinum sativum*
Parsley originated in the eastern Mediterranean and it was used in ancient Greece and Rome. It is the most popular herb around the Mediterranean and goes into almost everything. It is a good source of beta-carotene. The flat-leaved variety is the type used in the Mediterranean and it is considered to have much better flavour than the curly-leaved variety.

SAFFRON *Crocus sativus*
The golden-orange coloured threads of saffron are the dried stigmas of the autumnal purple-coloured flowers of the crocus plants. They make the most expensive aromatic ingredient in the world because both flowers and stigmas are hand-picked and it takes about 6,000 of them to produce 25 g / 1 oz of saffron. Jill Norman in her book *Spices* says that it was probably first cultivated in Asia Minor as it was used by the ancient Egyptians, Greeks and Romans.

The best saffron nowadays comes from Spain, where it was introduced by the Arabs around the tenth century. Saffron has an unmistakable aroma and a slightly bitter taste. A pinch of threads will colour a whole dish bright golden. It is preferable to buy threads to safeguard against adulteration.

OTHER FLAVOURING INGREDIENTS
ANCHOVIES
Slim, elongated, silvery-blue anchovies are prized throughout the Mediterranean, either fresh or salted. It is a cheap fish, but a gastronome's dream. The beloved *boquerones* of Spanish cuisine, the *hamsi* of Turkish and the *gavros* of Greek are baked with garlic, olive oil, lemon and oregano, or they are fried crisp.

They are ubiquitous around the Mediterranean in their salted form. Nowadays, however, they are more familiar as fillets preserved in brine in jars or in tins with olive oil. There is no doubt that the best are the dried salted ones, which should be rinsed properly before being used. People who object to the strong taste of anchovies occasionally first marinate them in milk and then rinse them.

Salted anchovies will liven up the most frugal of meals, which explains their popularity since ancient times. They are used in pizzas, with pasta, in salads such as Salade Niçoise (page 136), and pounded they make the French spread *anchoïade* and the Italian *bagna caôda.*

CAPERS
Capers grow wild all around the Mediterranean and they have been used there for thousands of years. The small pretty bush, which often appears to be trailing as it prefers to grow from high ground, has large pink flowers which resemble those of the lily or wild rose, and they are ephemeral – flowering in the morning and gone by the evening. On the Aegean island of Santorini, where they are proud of their capers, they

also pickle the young caper shoots and serve them with olive oil as a special *mezze* called *kaparofylla*. Capers can be either pickled in brine or dry-salted.

HARISSA

This North African condiment, traditionally served with couscous, is basically a chilli and garlic sauce and it can easily be made by puréeing chillies with garlic and some ground coriander seeds and cumin.

MASTIC

Mastic is the solid gum or resin from the bark of the evergreen tree *Pistacia lentiscus*, which grows mainly on the Greek island of Chios but also in some places in the Middle East. The word comes from the Greek word *masso* – to chew, hence to masticate.

Its flavour and aroma – like freshly ironed linen I think – is essential to a number of Greek breads and cakes. It is wonderful in ice-creams and used to be the traditional flavouring in Turkish delight.

RAS EL HANOUT

This is a formidable mixture of spices, herbs and dried flowers, in all about twenty-five of them, some with medicinal and others with aphrodisiac qualities, such as ash berries, monk's pepper and cantharides. Among other things it contains cinnamon, cardamom, cloves, turmeric, ginger, lavender flowers and cumin. Nowadays it is mostly bought ready-made in the markets. It is used in kebabs, couscous and rice dishes, and in tajines for its warming effect.

ROSE WATER

Roses originated probably in ancient Persia and Babylon. Persia apparently was exporting rose water and rose wine to distant places, such as China, two thousand years ago. It was the Persians and the Arabs who developed a taste for rose water, which they used not only for medicinal purposes, in perfumes and cosmetics but in all kinds of dishes, from pilaffs to desserts. Rose water came to Europe with the Crusaders. It is extracted from the petals either by steam distillation under pressure or water. According to food writer Helen Saberi, it takes thirty roses to produce one drop of oil or 60,000 roses for one ounce.

SUMAK

This is the sour red berries of a wild bush (*Rhus coriaria*) which grows all over the Middle East. They are dried to a deep burgundy colour for use either whole or ground. Sumak has a pleasantly mild but definite fruity sour taste and is sprinkled over fish, kebabs or salads such as Fattoush (page 138) to add another layer of flavour. Quite often chopped raw onions to accompany kebabs are first rolled in it.

TAHINA PASTE

Tahina paste is made from roasted pulped sesame seeds. It is used extensively in the Middle East in dishes such as Hummus (page 40) and *mezze* such as Tahinosalata (page 46). It is extremely nutritious.

VINEGAR

Vinegar is any alcoholic liquid which has become sour by the action of acid-forming bacteria. The word is derived from the French *vin aigre*, or sour wine. Vinegar made from fermented grape juice has been used in the Mediterranean since ancient times. Nowadays the two aristocrats of vinegar are the Italian balsamic and the Spanish sherry vinegar.

Balsamic is made mainly from Trebbiano grapes in Modena, with an ebony colour, a syrupy consistency and full spicy bouquet. This starts with fresh grape must, which is boiled down in order to concentrate the sugar content and flavour. A respectable balsamic vinegar should be aged in wood for at least six years (some say twelve) for its flavours to develop.

Spanish sherry vinegar, made in Jerez from the Palomino grapes, is dark and smooth with a rounded caramel taste, but it is not as sweet as balsamic.

NUTS

PINE NUTS

Pine nuts are the seeds contained inside the cones of a certain pine tree, the *Pinus pinea*, which is indigenous to the Mediterranean. Once the seeds have come out of the cone they have a woody skin like a pistachio nut, which has to be cracked in order to take the nut out. So, collecting pine nuts is very labour-intensive, which explains their high price. Their delicately sweet creamy, smooth taste combines so well with all kinds of ingredients, from vegetables to fruit and pasta, that they are one of the most important items in the store cupboard. They should, however, be bought in small quantities and stored in a cool dark dry spot, as they don't keep well and readily go rancid.

I prefer to toast them lightly first before use, as this gives them a nuttier flavour and a crisper texture. They are used in a number of sweet and savoury dishes in the Middle East, Turkey and North Africa. In the Lebanon, one finds them in almost every dish. Sprinkled over salads or fruit salads, toasted pine nuts add quite an exotic note. Although rich in calories, a few pine nuts go a long way.

PISTACHIO NUTS

These are the fruit of a rather small tree, *Pistacia vera*, and they appear in clusters in the spring. The inner kernel of a pistachio has a beautiful green colour and a very delicate nutty taste. The love for pistachios is proverbial in the Arab countries, where they are used as a filling for a number of honey-drenched desserts like *baklava*. They are a labour-intensive and fragile crop, and their price is correspondingly high. However, even a small quantity used in a dish will add an exquisite note. They are used in both sweet and savoury dishes: they are sprinkled over pilaffs in Middle Eastern countries and in Turkey; they are delicious sprinkled over ice-cream and fruit salads; and they are also used in Turkish delight or in mouthwatering caramelized clusters. The stout fleshy Persian pistachio nuts are among the best.

DAIRY PRODUCTS

FETA CHEESE

Greek Feta cheese is a soft but firm brilliantly white cheese made, ideally, from sheep's or goats' milk. It has a sharp, lightly salty taste and a sheepy fragrance, which I love. A good Feta is extremely appetising. In Greece it is ubiquitous, as it is served at all times of the day – for breakfast, for *mezze*, for lunch, at dinner, and in between for snacks as well. It is also crumbled and used in stuffings for pies, from cheese pies to courgette or spinach pies and over salads.

HALOUMI

Traditionally, Cypriot haloumi was made either from goats' or sheep's milk. Nowadays, haloumi is exported from Cyprus in two forms, the fresh variety and the hard or older variety. It is mostly made with a combination of primarily cows' milk and some sheep's milk. The fresh variety, which has a shorter shelf-life and is sold pre-packed, has an unmistakable elastic texture and a savoury salty taste. It is eaten fresh – it goes well with tomatoes – but it is at its best sliced and grilled, either over charcoal or on a ridged heavy cast-iron pan. It is also fried in olive oil and served as part of a *mezze*, or it may be fried with eggs.

If it is too salty first rinse it under cold water.

The older, matured variety is normally kept in brine in tins and sold by the weight. This cheese is fairly hard in texture and quite salty. It is mainly used grated over pasta dishes, with a little mint, and for a Cypriot version of ravioli as well as for grilling.

MOZZARELLA CHEESE

Mozzarella is ideally made from buffalos' milk and it has a rich sweet taste and a pleasing soft texture. Because of its melting qualities, it makes very good toppings for baked dishes and it is excellent combined with tomatoes – both characteristics combining memorably in that Italian classic, the pizza.

PARMESAN CHEESE

Parmesan is the best-known among Italian cheeses and one of the most tasty cheeses in the world. It is made mostly in Parma but also in Bologna and Modena. It is matured for between eighteen months and two years before going into the market and its production is governed by strict regulations. It should have a mellow rich flavour and a satisfying crumbly texture. The large wheels exported from Italy will always have the words 'Parmigiano-reggiano' printed on the side. When grated Parmesan is called for in a dish it is infinitely better to grate it freshly.

PECORINO

Pecorino is an Italian cheese made from ewes' milk – hence its name, *pecora* meaning sheep – which is produced in different regions of Italy and has different flavours, from soft, sweet and mellow to harder, more savoury and salty. The cheese made in Tuscany is called Pecorino Toscano and that from Sardinia Pecorino Sardo. Pecorino Romano, made in and around Rome, can be quite hard and a bit too salty.

The textures and tastes of the cheeses vary, firstly because of the feed on which the ewes will have been grazing, but more importantly because of its degree of maturity. The fresh variety can be between one and two months old and the harder and more pungent, saltier variety will be about six months old.

It is important to taste the cheese before buying it. For instance, when using it to make pesto, a fresher, milder variety would be best. For pasta fillings, such as the Chard Cannelloni with Pine Nuts on page 64, the harder, more mature variety is more suitable.

RICOTTA

Ricotta is a fresh white cheese made from whey and it should be soft, creamy and sweet-tasting. Because of its fresh character it should be used quickly as it is extremely perishable and acquires a sour taste and a yellow colour when old. It is extremely useful in stuffings, in sweets or served with fruit.

YOGHURT

Yoghurt is made by causing milk to ferment by the introduction of the active bacteria *lactobacillus bulgaricus* and *streptococcus thermophilus*. It was brought to the West by the Nomadic Turks and there are mentions of yoghurt in seventh-century texts.

Yoghurt is nourishing, it helps digestion, it is soothing to the nerves and it is believed to have therapeutic qualities, particularly for intestinal trouble. All in all, it is a general restorative. It is used daily in Turkey and the Middle East, where it will be found in many salads and dips. It is also popular in Greece, where a bowl of creamy yoghurt is often served with thick honey and topped with walnuts. In Turkey it is made into a cooling drink called *ayran*.

Yoghurt is rich in vitamins B_2 and B_{12}, also vitamin A if it is full-fat. It is also full of protein and calcium.

Breads &
Basics

SAVOURY OLIVE BREAD

This is a very unusual recipe which comes from my Greek-Cypriot friend Vera Kyriakou and which I haven't encountered anywhere else in this form. Freshly baked, these crusty rolls are magnificent; cold, they are unforgettably robust! They are excellent for a picnic but also good with drinks before dinner.

Once baked, they can be frozen, then allowed to defrost for a couple of hours before being warmed up in the oven. One word of warning: do not use sharp olives soaked in vinegar – such as the Greek Kalamata – but an oily or wrinkly type. The olives can be used with the stones, but do warn people.

MAKES *about 22 rolls*

PREPARATION *about 30 minutes, plus 45 minutes' proving*

COOKING *about 30 minutes*

Calories per serving *232*
Total fat *Medium*
Saturated fat *Low*
Protein *Low*
Carbohydrate *Medium*
Cholesterol *Nil*
Vitamins *Folate, A, E,*
Minerals *Calcium,*
Selenium, Potassium

450 G / 1 LB OILY OLIVES, PREFERABLY STONED
450 G / 1 LB FRESH SPINACH, TRIMMED
225 G / 8 OZ ONIONS, PEELED, OR
7-8 SPRING ONIONS, TRIMMED
LARGE HANDFUL OF FRESH CORIANDER, TRIMMED
25 G / 1 OZ FRESH YEAST

600 ML / 1 PINT WARM WATER
900 G / 2 LB PLAIN OR WHOLEMEAL FLOUR
150 ML / ¼ PINT OLIVE OIL
½ TEASPOON SALT
ABOUT 2 TABLESPOONS VEGETABLE OIL

1 If the olives have been kept in brine they will be extremely salty and will first have to be rinsed briefly. Chop the spinach, onions and coriander finely.

2 In a bowl, dissolve the yeast in half the warm water. Let it stand for 10 minutes. In another large bowl, mix the flour, olive oil and half of the salt and rub together. Add the yeast solution, mix well and knead with your knuckles for 10 minutes. Keep adding more of the warm water as necessary. You may not need all of it, even though the dough should be quite wet and sticky.

3 In a separate bowl, mix all the chopped greenery with the drained olives and remaining salt. Add to the dough, mix well and knead again until all is well incorporated.

4 Cover the dough with a clean tea towel and then a blanket, and let it rest in a warm place for about 45 minutes, or until it is well risen.

5 Preheat the oven to 220°C/425°F/gas 7. Oil a baking tray with a little vegetable oil and also oil your hands to prevent the dough from sticking to them. Form the dough into large rolls, about 8 cm / 3 in across. Arrange on the baking tray. (You can usually only fit a dozen at a time on a tray, so – as they have to be cooked in the middle of a conventional oven – you may have to cook in two batches; if you have a fan-assisted oven you can cook two trays at a time.) Keep oiling your hands while you are working.

6 Place the baking tray(s) in the oven and cook for 15 minutes. Then turn the heat down to 190°C/375°F/gas 5 and cook for another 15 minutes, until the rolls are nicely brown.

Clockwise from the left: Savoury Olive Bread, Tuscan Bread with Rosemary and Olive Oil (page 30), Pizza Napoletana (page 31)

TUSCAN BREAD WITH ROSEMARY AND OLIVE OIL

This is the recipe of my friend Cecile Harris, who is an inspirational cook and baker. She often made this bread for us when we stayed with her in Tuscany. There she had the luxury of an outdoor wood-burning oven which produced mouthwatering results. It is a very tasty bread but also easy to make, and delicious toasted. So it is a good candidate for bruschetta and crostini. Rosemary is the aroma one often encounters in breads from Tuscany, but Cecile makes it with all kinds of additions, such as sun-dried tomatoes or walnuts. One could also use half wholemeal flour and half white. Italian flour, which contains much more gluten, achieves the best results; it can be found in specialist shops and some supermarkets. (See page 29.)

MAKES *2 round loaves or 1 large one*

PREPARATION *about 30 minutes, plus 1¼-1½ hours' resting and proving*

COOKING *45-60 minutes*

Calories per serving *193*
Total fat *Low*
Saturated fat *Low*
Protein *Low*
Carbohydrate *High*
Cholesterol *Nil*
Vitamins *Folate, B₁*
Minerals *Iron, Selenium*

3-4 TABLESPOONS FRESH ROSEMARY NEEDLES, CHOPPED, OR 2 TABLESPOONS DRIED ROSEMARY
90 ML / 3 FL OZ OLIVE OIL, PLUS MORE FOR THE MOULD IF USING
600 ML / 1 PINT WARM WATER
25 G / 1 OZ FRESH YEAST
1 KG / 2¼ LB STRONG WHITE FLOUR, PLUS A LITTLE EXTRA FOR KNEADING AND DUSTING
25 G / 1 OZ SALT
LITTLE COARSE SEA SALT, FOR SPRINKLING

1 Place the water in a large bowl and dissolve the yeast in it. Leave for 10 minutes until frothy.
2 Add the flour, followed by the oil, salt and rosemary. Stir until it is all mixed together. Place the dough on a floured surface and knead by hand for 10 minutes, adding a little more flour as needed until it forms a smooth and elastic dough. Cover the dough and let it rest for 45 minutes in a warm place.
3 Punch the dough down a few times, flattening it, then divide it into two and either put each one in a lightly oiled rectangular 1.1 litre / 2 pint loaf tin or form each one into a loaf shape. Place them on a floured baking sheet and cover with a clean cloth. (A word of advice: if the weather is hot the dough tends to be loose and spreads all over the place, so it has to be contained. In such a case the loaf tin is the best solution or you can put a ring around each loaf to contain it.) Let the dough rise for 30-40 minutes in a warm place.
4 Preheat the oven to 230°C/450°F/gas 8. Steam is essential for a crusty loaf, so put a dish of boiling water on the lower shelf of the oven. Sprinkle the sea salt on top of the dough just before baking and bake for 45-60 minutes. To see if a loaf is done, take it out of any mould being used and tap it at the base; it should sound hollow. If it isn't ready, place it back on the baking sheet upside down – without any tin – and bake a little longer. Let the loaf cool on a wire rack.

PIZZA

Traditionally pizza is baked on a brick or stone surface in a wood-fired oven, so the dough becomes crisp with the intense heat. The best alternative is to use a baking stone. (See page 29.)

115 G / 4 OZ STRONG WHITE FLOUR
115 G / 4 OZ WHOLEMEAL FLOUR
1 TEASPOON SALT
1 TEASPOON EASY-BLEND YEAST
150 ML / ¼ PINT WARM WATER
1 TABLESPOON OLIVE OIL

FOR PIZZA MARGHERITA:
2 TABLESPOONS OLIVE OIL
550 G / 1¼ LB RIPE TOMATOES, TRIMMED AND SLICED IN THICK WEDGES, OR 400 G / 14 OZ CANNED TOMATOES, DRAINED
1 TEASPOON EACH DRIED OREGANO AND THYME

150 G / 5 OZ MOZZARELLA CHEESE, COARSELY GRATED
2 TABLESPOONS GRATED PARMESAN CHEESE
SALT AND FRESHLY GROUND BLACK PEPPER

FOR PIZZA NAPOLETANA:
550 G / 1¼ LB RIPE TOMATOES, TRIMMED AND SLICED IN THICK WEDGES, OR 400 G / 14 OZ CANNED TOMATOES, DRAINED
1 TEASPOON EACH DRIED OREGANO AND THYME
FEW TORN BASIL LEAVES
5-6 ANCHOVY FILLETS, CUT INTO PIECES
1 TABLESPOON OLIVE OIL
8-10 SMALL BLACK OLIVES

SERVES *4-6*

PREPARATION *about 30 minutes, plus 30 minutes' proving*

COOKING *about 30 minutes*

Calories per serving *268*
Total fat *Medium*
Saturated fat *Medium*
Protein *Medium*
Carbohydrate *Low*
Cholesterol *11 mg*
Vitamins *A, C, E, B group*
Minerals *Iron, Zinc, Selenium, Calcium, Potassium*

1 Put the flours in a bowl and mix in salt and yeast. Add the water and oil and mix with a knife to a soft dough. Knead for 5 minutes on a floured surface. Cover and leave 5 minutes.

2 Knead the dough again on a floured surface for 3-4 minutes until soft and elastic. With the use of a rolling pin and by pulling and stretching by hand, shape the dough into either a large oblong shape or a 28 cm / 11 in round. It should be very thin, about 5 mm / ¼ in, and with a slightly raised rim. Place the dough on an oiled baking sheet, cover and leave to rise for 30 minutes in the kitchen.

3 Preheat the oven to 230°C/450°F/gas 8 at least 20 minutes ahead of cooking. If you have a baking stone, place it in the upper shelf of the oven and preheat it too. Add any favourite topping just before the pizza is to be baked, otherwise it will become soggy.

4 To make Pizza Margherita: heat the oil in a frying pan, add the tomatoes and turn with a spatula for 2-3 minutes over moderate heat. Add herbs and salt and cook for 5-6 minutes more, stirring occasionally, until fresh tomatoes look wilted and most of the liquid has evaporated. Lift the tomatoes out with a slotted spoon, leaving excess juices behind, and spread evenly over the pizza. Sprinkle Mozzarella on top, followed by Parmesan.

5 To make Pizza Napoletana: prepare the tomatoes as above and spread them evenly on the dough. Sprinkle over the basil and then add the anchovy. Sprinkle the olive oil on top and scatter over the black olives.

6 Bake either pizza for 15 minutes on the upper shelf of the oven, placing it directly on the stone if you are using one, until the dough appears crisp and golden.

SALSA DI POMODORO
Italian Tomato Sauce

This is the queen of the standby sauces as it can be made quickly and is very versatile. Its main role is with pasta of any kind, or with polenta. The list of potential uses is, however, much more varied than this. It can be spread over potatoes or other vegetables and baked in the oven like a gratin. It can be spread over steaks of fish, such as cod, or over whole mackerel and baked in the oven as is done in Greece and in Turkey. Alternatively, you can beat 3-4 eggs and combine them with some of this sauce, then cook the mixture like scrambled eggs and you instantly have a version of the Greek strapatsatha, *from the island of Corfu. For a North African flavour, spread some of this sauce in a frying pan, break 4 whole eggs on top, sprinkle some paprika and ground cumin on each egg, cover and cook slowly until set.*

When I make this as a pasta sauce for 4 people, I use two tins of tomatoes so that the pasta is lusciously coated. I find one tin is a little mean. We are only talking about tins of tomatoes after all and whatever is not used will wait in a refrigerator for about 4 days, or it can be frozen. I also liquidize the tomatoes first as I find the velvety consistency of the sauce much more appealing, but you don't have to do that if in a hurry – simply use tins of ready-chopped tomatoes. Of course the sauce can be made with fresh tomatoes, as we do in the summer, and then it becomes totally captivating. You will need at least 1 kg / 2 lb (or more) ripe tomatoes, peeled, seeded and chopped and cooked a little longer.

MAKES *about 600 ml / 1 pint*

PREPARATION *10 minutes*

COOKING *about 40 minutes*

Calories per serving *112*
Total fat *High*
Saturated fat *Low*
Protein *Low*
Carbohydrate *Low*
Cholesterol *Nil*
Vitamins *B₆, E*
Minerals *Iron, Potassium*

2 (400 G/14 OZ) TINS OF TOMATOES (WITH THEIR LIQUID), LIQUIDIZED
1 TABLESPOON TOMATO PASTE
2-3 TABLESPOONS OLIVE OIL
1 MEDIUM ONION, FINELY CHOPPED
2 GARLIC CLOVES, CHOPPED
1 TEASPOON DRIED OREGANO
½ TEASPOON DEMERARA (OR WHITE) SUGAR
LITTLE HOT WATER
3-4 SPRIGS OF FRESH BASIL, TORN BY HAND, OR 3 TABLESPOONS CHOPPED PARSLEY
SALT AND FRESHLY GROUND BLACK PEPPER

1 Heat the oil gently in a medium saucepan and sauté the onion until translucent. Add the garlic and oregano and, as soon as the garlic aroma rises, add the tomatoes, sugar and some seasoning.

2 Cover the mixture and cook gently for 15 minutes, stirring occasionally. Add the tomato paste and cook for 15 more minutes, adding a little hot water if needed. Stir the sauce often at this stage in case it sticks. It should be quite smooth and thick by the end.

3 Remove the thickened sauce from the heat and mix in the torn fresh basil or chopped parsley.

PESTO

A book on Mediterranean food cannot be complete without a recipe for delicious pesto. It is the most wonderful sauce ever invented and we owe it to the Genoese. It is they who specify that for proper pesto the small-leaved variety of basil is the best and my grandmother, although she had never heard of – or made – pesto in her time always maintained that the small-leaved variety, which she kept on every windowsill and in the garden, was superior.

Pesto may be used with any pasta, although it works best with large flat ribbons like fettuccine or tubular pasta such as penne, which will hold larger quantities of the sauce. On the other hand, in the summer when basil is plentiful I tend to serve it with almost everything – with courgettes, with potato salad, with soup, with rice pilaff, and so on. (See page 35.)

50 G / 2 OZ BASIL LEAVES
1 LARGE GARLIC CLOVE, PEELED AND CHOPPED
1½ TABLESPOONS PINE NUTS
3 TABLESPOONS OLIVE OIL

25 G / 1 OZ PARMESAN CHEESE, FRESHLY GRATED
1 TABLESPOON FRESHLY GRATED PECORINO SARDO OR ROMANO CHEESE

1 Place all the ingredients except the cheeses in a food processor and give it a quick burst. Stop and scrape everything down and repeat. If the sauce appears too dry, add 1 tablespoon of water.
2 When the sauce has a creamy appearance, add both the grated cheeses and give it one more rapid burst.
3 Keep the sauce refrigerated until needed. Just before using it, dilute it a little by adding either 2 tablespoons of the hot pasta cooking water or just plain warm water.

MAKES *175 g / 6½ oz*

PREPARATION *5-10 minutes*

Calories per tablespoon *45*
Total fat *High*
Saturated fat *High*
Protein *Low*
Carbohydrate *Low*
Cholesterol *3 mg*
Vitamins *A, E*
Minerals *Calcium, Iron, Zinc, Potassium*

SARIMSAKLI YOGHURT
Yoghurt and Garlic Sauce

As it can be made easily and speedily, this sauce from Turkey is a good standby. It can be served not only with vegetables and pulses but also with meat dishes, and it always adds one more appetizing aspect to the meal.

200 G / 7 OZ THICK LOW-FAT NATURAL YOGHURT
2 GARLIC CLOVES, CRUSHED

5-6 MINT LEAVES, FINELY CHOPPED
PINCH OF PAPRIKA, TO GARNISH (OPTIONAL)

1 Beat the yoghurt and garlic together in a bowl. Mix in the mint, cover and refrigerate.
2 Serve lightly chilled, garnished with a little paprika if you wish.

MAKES *250 g / 8 oz*

PREPARATION *5 minutes, plus chilling*

Calories per tablespoon *9*
Total fat *Low*
Saturated fat *Low*
Protein *High*
Carbohydrate *Medium*
Cholesterol *1 mg*
Vitamins *Negligible*
Minerals *Iodine, Calcium*

SKORTHALIA

In Greek island homes this garlic sauce is indispensable in order to liven up a frugal meal of boiled vegetables, fried fish or, particularly, salt cod or fried vegetables. Skorthalia has been consumed in Greece since ancient times. It also appears all over the Mediterranean under different names, such as tarator *in Turkey and the Middle East, the Italian* agliata *and the French* aïoli, *although that contains eggs.*

MAKES *about 175 g / 6½ oz*

PREPARATION *10 minutes, plus 10 minutes' soaking*

Calories per tablespoon *117*
Total fat *High*
Saturated fat *Low*
Protein *Low*
Carbohydrate *Low*
Cholesterol *Nil*
Vitamins *Folate, E*
Minerals *Calcium, Iron, Zinc*

2-3 GARLIC CLOVES, CHOPPED
3 MEDIUM SLICES OF CRUSTLESS BREAD, SOAKED IN WATER FOR 10 MINUTES
1 TABLESPOON WHITE WINE VINEGAR

2 TABLESPOONS OLIVE OIL
50 G / 2 OZ GROUND WALNUTS OR ALMONDS (OPTIONAL)
SALT
PINCH OF PAPRIKA, TO GARNISH (OPTIONAL)

1 Squeeze most of the water from the bread. Place it in a liquidizer with the garlic, vinegar and salt to taste. Then blend until smooth.
2 With the machine still running, dribble in the oil. Add the nuts, if they are used, and blend briefly. The sauce should be runny.
3 Serve garnished with a little paprika if you wish.

ROUILLE

The rouille *which accompanies Provençal fish soups, particularly* Bouillabaisse, *is a fiery orange-coloured kind of mayonnaise made with garlic and chilli. It is spread on croutons and these are floated on top of, or mixed into, the soup. A substantial amount of olive oil is usually needed for this sauce, but I have cut the amount down and used instead some bread and ground nuts as thickening agents.*

MAKES *about 175 g / 6½ oz*

PREPARATION *5-10 minutes, plus soaking*

Calories per tablespoon *96*
Total fat *High*
Saturated fat *Medium*
Protein *Low*
Carbohydrate *Low*
Cholesterol *31 mg*
Vitamins *A, B₁₂*
Minerals *Iron*

1 FRESH OR DRIED RED CHILLI, SEEDED AND CHOPPED
1 MEDIUM CRUSTLESS SLICE OF BREAD, SOAKED IN WATER FOR 10 MINUTES
2 GARLIC CLOVES, CHOPPED
1 EGG YOLK

1 TABLESPOON GROUND ALMONDS
1 TEASPOON TOMATO PASTE
½ TEASPOON EACH PAPRIKA AND CAYENNE PEPPER
4 TABLESPOONS OLIVE OIL
SALT

1 If using a dried chilli, first soak it in a little boiling water for 30 minutes.
2 Place the chilli in a food processor (if dried add a little of its liquid). Squeeze excess water from the bread and add it in together with the remaining ingredients apart from the oil. Add salt to taste. Process to a smooth paste.
3 With the machine still running, dribble in the oil slowly to form a thick and creamy sauce. If it is too solid, add a little cold water.
4 Taste the sauce (it should be fiery) and adjust the seasoning with more salt and cayenne.

Clockwise from the top: Skorthalia, Pesto (page 33), Rouille

AVGOLEMONO

MAKES *about 300 ml / ½ pint*

PREPARATION *about 5 minutes*

Calories per tablespoon *11*
Total fat *High*
Saturated fat *High*
Protein *High*
Carbohydrate *Low*
Cholesterol *25 mg*
Vitamins *B₁₂*
Minerals *Iron, Zinc*

This is the delicious egg-and-lemon sauce which transforms casseroles and soups in Greece. It can be added to more or less anything – meat, fish or vegetables.

2 LARGE EGGS AT ROOM TEMPERATURE | **1 TABLESPOON CORNFLOUR MIXED IN A LITTLE WATER**
JUICE OF 2 LEMONS

1 In a bowl, beat the eggs lightly with a fork or balloon whisk. Add the lemon juice and the cornflour, then beat together until smooth.
2 Add 2-3 small ladlefuls of liquid from the dish it is to enrich, beating together for 1 minute between each addition. By now the sauce will be warm so you can pour it slowly into the dish, off the heat, stirring vigorously.
3 Warm the dish up over very, very gentle heat, otherwise the eggs may curdle, although the cornflour will safeguard against that for a minute or so. Serve immediately.

BÉCHAMEL SAUCE

This is quite a thin béchamel as it is intended mainly for the Cannelloni on page 64, where it will be baked for a long time and thicken. Whenever a thicker sauce is required, add a little more flour.

MAKES *about 1 litre / 1¾ pints*
PREPARATION *5-10 minutes*

COOKING *about 40 minutes*

Calories per serving *187*
Total fat *Medium*
Saturated fat *Medium*
Protein *Medium*
Carbohydrate *Low*
Cholesterol *71 mg*
Vitamins *A, B group*
Minerals *Calcium, Zinc, Iodine, Potassium*

40 G / 1½ OZ BUTTER | **2 TABLESPOONS GRATED PARMESAN CHEESE**
50 G / 2 OZ PLAIN FLOUR | **1 EGG, LIGHTLY BEATEN**
850 ML / 1½ PINTS HOT SEMI-SKIMMED MILK | **SALT AND FRESHLY GROUND BLACK OR WHITE PEPPER**
2 PINCHES OF FRESHLY GRATED NUTMEG

1 In a heavy-based saucepan melt the butter gently over very low heat. Add the flour gradually, stirring constantly with a wooden spatula. I add a couple of tablespoons of milk if the mixture looks too solid.
2 Once all the flour is in, stir for 1 more minute without letting it brown. Withdraw from the heat and start adding the milk gradually, 2-3 tablespoons at a time, stirring constantly until it has been fully blended. This safeguards against the formation of lumps. Return to a gentle heat and as you go on you can add a little more milk each time.
3 When all the milk has been added, season to taste. Then simmer over a low heat, stirring constantly, for another 10 minutes until the sauce has thickened enough to coat a spoon. The whole process takes about half an hour.
4 Remove the sauce from the heat and let it stand for 5 minutes. Then add the nutmeg, the Parmesan and the egg, stirring constantly until well incorporated. Adjust the seasoning, if necessary. If the sauce is going to stand a little, keep stirring it from time to time to prevent a skin forming on top, or cut a piece of cling film and fit it snugly on the surface.

STOCKS

Stocks are indispensable in the making of certain dishes such as soups or risotti. They constitute the magic ingredient which can transform a dish, so they are worth making, particularly since they can be prepared in advance and kept in the freezer. I am not going to give exact quantities, but simply indicate instead what the ingredients are and how they are cooked.

VEGETABLE STOCK

For vegetable stock you will need a selection of vegetables such as onions, carrots, leeks, celery, courgettes and a potato or two. Basically anything goes. Trim or peel each vegetable as necessary and coarsely chop them. Put them in a pan and add water to cover them completely. Add some seasoning (whole peppercorns are good for stock instead of ground pepper as they can be strained off), bring to the boil and simmer gently for about 40-50 minutes. Strain and discard the vegetables or use for a purée. If not using the stock immediately, it may be kept in the fridge for 3-4 days, or frozen.

CHICKEN STOCK

For a really good flavour, this must be made with a fresh chicken, particularly an older boiling fowl, or it can be made with wings and necks. If using a whole chicken, this should be cut into 4-6 pieces. Barely cover the chicken pieces with cold water, bring to the boil and skim until clear. Add some coarsely chopped carrots, onions and celery, some seasoning, 1-2 bay leaves and a small bunch of fresh herbs such as oregano, thyme or marjoram. Cook gently for 1 hour or a little longer. Strain and use the chicken for a separate meal. When cool, lift off the thin layer of fat from the surface before use.

MEAT STOCK

Ask your butcher to give you some fresh beef or veal bones, including 1 or 2 pieces of marrow bone. Rinse the bones and proceed as for chicken stock, but cook for 1½ hours.

FISH STOCK

Fishmongers will readily provide a selection of fresh trimmings (you probably need about 1 kg / 2 lb) from larger fish (which should include bones, but also heads), particularly if you give them notice. Ask them not to include oily fish. Rinse everything and proceed as in the recipe for chicken stock, but cook for only 30 minutes (and no more, otherwise it may become bitter).

Mezze
& Soups

HUMMUS

This Middle Eastern chickpea dip can liven up any table with its robust and earthy tastes. It could accompany a simple vegetable casserole or soup, or it could hold its place as part of a larger mezze table.

SERVES 6-8

PREPARATION *15 minutes, plus overnight soaking*

COOKING *about 1½ hours*

Calories per serving *133*
Total fat *High*
Saturated fat *Low*
Protein *Medium*
Carbohydrate *Low*
Cholesterol *Nil*
Vitamins *A, B group*
Minerals *Calcium, Zinc, Iodine, Potassium*

175 G / 6 OZ CHICKPEAS, PICKED CLEAN AND SOAKED IN COLD WATER OVERNIGHT
2 TABLESPOONS TAHINA PASTE
2 GARLIC CLOVES, PEELED AND CHOPPED
JUICE OF 1-2 LEMONS
2 TEASPOONS GROUND CUMIN

1 TABLESPOON OLIVE OIL
SALT AND FRESHLY GROUND PEPPER

TO DRESS:
1 TEASPOON OLIVE OIL
½ TEASPOON PAPRIKA OR A LITTLE CAYENNE PEPPER

1 Rinse the chickpeas, place in a saucepan and cover with plenty of water. Bring to the boil and skim until clear. Cover and boil the chickpeas until perfectly soft. This can take about 1½ hours (or about 20 minutes if using a pressure cooker). Drain, reserving the cooking liquid.

2 If the tahina paste appears separated in the jar, first mix it properly with a fork. Divide all the ingredients into two batches and place the first one in a food processor with 150 ml / ¼ pint of the chickpea cooking liquid. Process until grainy and of a runny consistency. Add a little more of the cooking liquid if necessary. Taste and adjust seasoning, then blend again briefly. Empty out on a pretty flat platter and repeat with the remaining ingredients.

3 Drizzle a little oil over the hummus and sprinkle the paprika or cayenne on top. Serve lightly chilled or at room temperature.

YOGHURT AND CUCUMBER SALAD

This is the sauce found all over the Eastern Mediterranean. Cacik to the Turks or tzatziki to the Greeks, it can be served with vegetable- and oil-based dishes, with raw vegetables, grilled fish or meat, roasts and salads.

SERVES 4-6

PREPARATION *10 minutes, plus chilling*

Calories per serving *51*
Total fat *High*
Saturated fat *Low*
Protein *High*
Carbohydrate *Low*
Cholesterol *2 mg*
Vitamins *B₂, B₃*
Minerals *Calcium, Iodine*

225 G / 8 OZ THICK PLAIN LOW-FAT YOGHURT
10 CM / 4 IN CUCUMBER, PEELED AND GRATED
1 TABLESPOON OLIVE OIL
1 TEASPOON WINE VINEGAR

1 GARLIC CLOVE, PEELED AND CRUSHED
1 TABLESPOON FINELY CHOPPED FRESH MINT, PLUS MORE LEAVE TO GARNISH
SALT

1 Whisk the oil, vinegar and garlic in a bowl. Add yoghurt and salt and beat until smooth.

2 Squeeze the cucumber with your hands to remove excess moisture, then mix it into the sauce with the mint. Cover and refrigerate.

3 Serve lightly chilled, garnished with mint.

Clockwise from the left: Hummus, Muhammara (page 42), Yoghurt and Cucumber Salad

MUHAMMARA
Turkish Walnut and Pepper Dip

This is a speciality of Gaziantep in South-east Turkey. There they would include a red pepper paste which the matriarch of each household makes at the end of the summer and stores for the winter. As this is almost impossible to obtain commercially, I have substituted pomegranate syrup (see page 19) for that additional twist in flavour. You can make it lower in fat and calories by omitting the pistachio and pine nuts. This recipe is based on one by my friend Holly Chase, an expert on all things Turkish. (See page 41.)

SERVES 6-8

PREPARATION *about 30 minutes, plus 2-3 hours' chilling*

Calories per serving *359*
Total fat *High*
Saturated fat *Low*
Protein *Low*
Carbohydrate *Low*
Cholesterol *Nil*
Vitamins *A, B₁, B₃, B₆, Folate, C, E,*
Minerals *Potassium, Iron, Zinc, Selenium*

150 G / 5½ OZ SHELLED WALNUTS, TOASTED IN A LOW OVEN FOR 10 MINUTES

3 RIPE RED PEPPERS, DESEEDED AND CHOPPED

3 MEDIUM SLICES OF BREAD (CRUSTS ET AL), TOASTED

1 GARLIC CLOVE, CRUSHED

RIND AND JUICE OF 1 UNCOATED LEMON

2 TABLESPOONS POMEGRANATE SYRUP (OPTIONAL)

1 TEASPOON NOT-TOO-HOT PEPPER FLAKES

OR 1 SMALL GREEN CHILLI, DESEEDED (OPTIONAL)

5-6 SPRIGS OF FLAT-LEAVED PARSLEY

6-7 MINT LEAVES

3 TABLESPOONS FRUITY OLIVE OIL

50 G / 2 OZ UNSALTED SHELLED PISTACHIO NUTS (OPTIONAL)

50 G / 2 OZ PINE NUTS, LIGHTLY TOASTED

SALT

1 Combine the bread and cooled walnuts in a food processor and reduce them to crumbs.
2 Add the chopped peppers, garlic, lemon rind and juice, pomegranate syrup and pepper flakes or chilli, if using. Process together to a pulp.
3 Add the herbs (reserving a few sprigs of parsley for garnish) and, with the machine still running, add the oil in a steady trickle.
4 Add salt to taste and the pistachio nuts if

using. Process with a quick burst so that the nuts are coarsely chopped and not powdered.
5 Chill for a couple of hours in order to let all the flavours blend together. Take out of the refrigerator about half an hour before serving.
6 Just before serving, mix in half of the pine nuts and turn out on a serving plate. Sprinkle the remaining pine nuts over to serve and garnish with a sprig of parsley if you wish.

BESSARA
Egyptian Purée of Broad Beans and Herbs

I was introduced to bessara by the Egyptian chef Esmat Farid of the restaurant Valley of the Kings in West London. I was instantly captivated by its lively refreshing taste. It is one of the ancient Arab dishes to be found from Egypt to Cyprus to North Africa under slightly different names such as byesar.

225 G / 8 OZ SKINNED DRIED BROAD BEANS, PICKED CLEAN AND SOAKED OVERNIGHT IN COLD WATER
50 G / 2 OZ EACH PARSLEY (PREFERABLY FLAT-LEAVED) AND CORIANDER, COARSELY CHOPPED
1-2 FRESH GREEN CHILLIES, DESEEDED AND CHOPPED
2 GARLIC CLOVES, CHOPPED
1½ TEASPOONS GROUND CUMIN
3 TABLESPOONS OLIVE OIL
1 MEDIUM ONION, PEELED AND THINLY SLICED
SALT

1 Strain and rinse the beans. Place in a pan, preferably a pressure cooker, with plenty of water and bring to the boil. Boil for 3-4 minutes and drain. Cover with fresh water by about 2.5 cm / 1 in and cook until done. In a pressure cooker this would take 10-15 minutes, otherwise it will take about 1 hour.
2 Mix in the herbs, cover and simmer for 5 minutes. Strain, reserving some of the liquid.
3 Combine the beans with the chillies, garlic, cumin, 2 tablespoons of oil and 3-4 tablespoons of the reserved liquid in a food processor and process to a smooth paste. Season to taste with salt. If too dry, add a little more of the cooking liquid. Empty into a medium-sized pâté dish, cover and refrigerate.
4 Just before serving, heat the remaining oil in a non-stick pan and fry the onion briskly until golden and crisp. Spread over the pâté and serve with fresh bread.

SERVES 4

PREPARATION *about 15 minutes, plus overnight soaking*

COOKING *about 1¼ hours, plus cooling*

Calories per serving *230*
Total fat *Medium*
Saturated fat *Low*
Protein *High*
Carbohydrate *Low*
Cholesterol *Nil*
Vitamins *A, B₁, B₂, B₃, B₆, Folate, C, E*
Minerals *Calcium, Iron, Zinc, Potassium*

MELITZANOSALATA

Melitzanosalata *in Greece and* baba ghanoush *in the Middle East are deliciously refreshing salads. Ideally the aubergines should be grilled on charcoal in order to give them that unmistakable smoky aroma. Here I have improvised a trick which produces at least some of the smoky flavour in the kitchen.*

1 KG / 2 LB 4 OZ LARGE AUBERGINES
½ SMALL ONION, COARSELY CHOPPED
1-2 GARLIC CLOVES, CRUSHED
JUICE OF 1 SMALL LEMON
3 TABLESPOONS OLIVE OIL
SALT AND FRESHLY GROUND BLACK PEPPER
2 TABLESPOONS CHOPPED FLAT-LEAVED PARSLEY
4-6 BLACK OLIVES, TO GARNISH

1 Preheat the oven to 180°C/350°F/gas 4. Prick the aubergines with a fork and lay them directly on the oven shelves and roast for about 1 hour, until soft and properly cooked. Turn them round twice during the process.
2 Wearing oven gloves, take the aubergines out of the oven and lay each one over a low naked flame for a 2-3 minutes, turning them as they become charred. This is messy, but does impart that smoky flavour. You can omit it altogether or do it for a shorter time.
3 Slit the cooled aubergines open. Spoon the flesh out into a strainer and squeeze it dry.
4 Place the flesh in a food processor with the onion, garlic and lemon juice and process rapidly. With the machine still running, dribble the oil in until a smooth paste is formed. Adjust the seasoning.
5 Spread on a serving platter, sprinkle parsley on top and pile olives in the middle.

SERVES 4

PREPARATION *about 10 minutes*

COOKING *about 1¼ hours, plus cooling*

Calories per serving *127*
Total fat *High*
Saturated fat *Medium*
Protein *Low*
Carbohydrate *Low*
Cholesterol *Nil*
Vitamins *B₃, Folate, C, E*
Minerals *Iron, Potassium*

ROAST COURGETTES WITH SALSA VERDE

Roasting courgettes transforms their flavour, as it concentrates it and they become much sweeter as a result. The green sauce with which they are served I make with a number of different fresh herbs and, of course, this gives scope for individual improvisation. This dish is extremely enticing when served with Italian bread, such as ciabatta or focaccia, or even a sourdough or French baguette.

Inspired by Anna Del Conte's wonderful book Entertaining all'Italiana *I have also treated aubergines in a very similar way to make* melanzane con salsa verde. *Top and tail them, cut them into rounds about 5 mm / ¼ in thick and place these slices side by side in one layer on the baking sheet. Season the olive oil and brush the aubergines sparingly with it. Cook in the oven as below for 35-40 minutes, until the aubergine slices are soft and starting to turn golden on top. Arrange them decoratively on a pretty serving platter and, about half an hour before serving, cover the top of each aubergine slice with a thin layer of the salsa verde. This makes an appetizing dish which is ideal for a buffet table or for serving cold at an* al fresco *lunch. To make a complete meal, they can be served with the Couscous Salad with Peaches, Rocket and Pine Nuts on page 83.*

SERVES *4-6*

PREPARATION *15-20 minutes*

COOKING *50 minutes, plus cooling*

Calories per serving *72*
Total fat *High*
Saturated fat *Medium*
Protein *Low*
Carbohydrate *Low*
Cholesterol *Nil*
Vitamins *A, C, Folate*
Minerals *Iron, Potassium*

675 G / 1½ LB MEDIUM-SIZED FIRM COURGETTES, TRIMMED BUT KEPT WHOLE
1 TABLESPOON OLIVE OIL

FOR THE SALSA VERDE:
2 GARLIC CLOVES, PEELED AND CHOPPED
1 TABLESPOON DIJON MUSTARD
LARGE HANDFUL OF FLAT-LEAVED PARSLEY
SMALL HANDFUL OF FRESH MINT
JUICE OF ½ LEMON
2-3 TABLESPOONS OLIVE OIL
SALT

1 Preheat the oven to 190°C/375°F/gas 5. Cover a baking sheet with foil, oil it lightly and arrange the courgettes on it. Brush their tops with a little oil and roast for 50 minutes.

2 Take the courgettes out of the oven and, when they are a little cooler, slice them across into 6 cm / 2½ in long pieces. Then, unless they are very slim, quarter each piece lengthwise to produce thin batons. Place the pieces in a large bowl.

3 While the courgettes are cooling, make the salsa: place all the ingredients, apart from the olive oil and a sprig or two of mint, in a food processor with salt to taste and work into a smooth paste. With the machine still running, slowly add in the olive oil and blend until well emulsified to a thick pesto-like sauce.

4 Shortly before the salad is to be served, add the sauce to the courgettes and toss gently to coat them. Garnish with the remaining mint.

Roast Courgettes with Salsa Verde

MARINATED MOZZARELLA WITH BARBA NIKOS'S FIG SLICES

This is an exotic personal improvisation which we serve at our Greek island home in the summer. Of course, we lack the Mozzarella there so we have to substitute Feta. We have this dish as a first course in the middle of August, when the figs on our trees are at their fullest. Even better when our elderly friend Barba Nikos arrives with presents from his majestic hundred-year-old fig tree.

SERVES *4*

PREPARATION *10 minutes, plus 2-4 hours' marinating*

Calories per serving *220*
Total fat *High*
Saturated fat *High*
Protein *Medium*
Carbohydrate *Low*
Cholesterol *24 mg*
Vitamins *A, B2, B12, E*
Minerals *Calcium, Zinc, Potassium*

150 G / 5 OZ BUFFALO MOZZARELLA CHEESE
5-6 FIRM FIGS
6-8 MINT LEAVES
SALT AND FRESHLY GROUND BLACK PEPPER

FOR THE MARINADE:
2 TABLESPOONS WALNUT OIL
1 TEASPOON SUNFLOWER OIL
JUICE OF 1 LEMON
½ GARLIC CLOVE, PEELED AND CRUSHED

1 Slice the cheese very thinly. Beat the marinade ingredients lightly together in a bowl and season to taste. Coat the cheese slices in it, cover and chill for 2-4 hours.
2 Just before serving, take the cheese out of the refrigerator. Trim both ends of each fig and slice each one in about 3-4 round slices. Arrange the cheese and fig slices decoratively on a round platter.
3 Dribble the marinade all over and scatter the mint on top.

TAHINOSALATA

Tahina is made from crushed sesame seeds and brings an exotic taste to anything to which it is added. Tahinosalata is a sharp and appetizing dip to be offered with vegetable crudités or hot pitta bread.

SERVES *4-6*

PREPARATION *10 minutes*

Calories per serving *90*
Total fat *High*
Saturated fat *Medium*
Protein *Low*
Carbohydrate *Low*
Cholesterol *Nil*
Vitamins *B1, B3, Folate*
Minerals *Iron, Calcium*

4 TABLESPOONS TAHINA PASTE
150 ML / ¼ PINT WARM WATER
2 GARLIC CLOVES, CHOPPED
½ TEASPOON GROUND CUMIN

1-2 TABLESPOONS OLIVE OIL
JUICE OF 1 LEMON
SALT
BLACK OLIVES, TO GARNISH

1 If the tahina paste in the jar looks separated, stir to mix it. Measure the paste, water, garlic and cumin into a food processor or blender. Season and mix briefly.
2 With the machine still running, start slowly adding the olive oil and lemon juice alternately, until the mixture looks creamy.
3 Adjust the seasoning and empty into a bowl. Garnish with the olives and serve. It will keep, covered, in the refrigerator for 3-4 days.

Marinated Mozzarella with Barba Nikos's Fig Slices

TYROPITAKIA LEFTERITSAS

These little cheese pies used to be made for us by an Athenian friend called Eleftheria, meaning 'liberty'. Hence their name. Cold, the pies are ideal for picnics.

FOR THE PASTRY:

200 G / 7 OZ SELF-RAISING FLOUR, SIFTED

2 TABLESPOONS OLIVE OIL

1 TABLESPOON MELTED BUTTER

85 G / 3 OZ PLAIN THICK LOW-FAT YOGHURT

1 TEASPOON VEGETABLE OIL , TO GREASE THE TIN

1 EGG YOLK, LIGHTLY BEATEN, TO GLAZE

FOR THE FILLING:

150 G / 5 OZ FETA CHEESE, CRUMBLED WITH A FORK

1 LARGE EGG, LIGHTLY BEATEN

2 TABLESPOONS FINELY CHOPPED DILL OR MINT

1 SPRING ONION, FINELY CHOPPED

FRESHLY GROUND BLACK PEPPER

MAKES *12-15*

PREPARATION *about 35 minutes, plus 15 minutes' resting*

COOKING *20 minutes,*

Calories per pie *108*
Total fat *High*
Saturated fat *High*
Protein *Low*
Carbohydrate *Low*
Cholesterol *39 mg*
Vitamins *B group*
Minerals *Calcium, Iron, Iodine*

1 Put the pastry ingredients into a bowl and mix with your hands. Add a little more flour if the mixture is too wet. Cover and rest in the refrigerator for 15 minutes.
2 Preheat the oven to 190°C/375°F/gas 5 and grease a baking sheet with the vegetable oil. In another bowl, combine the filling ingredients.
3 On a lightly-floured surface, roll out one-third of the pastry not too thinly. Using a glass or pastry cutter, cut out 8 cm / 3 in circles.
4 Place a teaspoon of filling along the middle of each pastry disc, then fold it over to make a small half-moon shape. Press the edges together to seal them. Place the pies on the baking sheet. Continue with the remaining pastry and filling until they are all used up.
5 Brush the tops with egg yolk and bake for 20 minutes, until golden. Serve hot or cold.

TAPENADE
Provençal Olive and Caper Paste

225 G / 8 OZ BLACK OLIVES, STONED (ABOUT 175 G / 6 OZ READY-STONED)

2 TABLESPOONS CAPERS, STRAINED AND RINSED

1 GARLIC CLOVE, PEELED AND CHOPPED

3 ANCHOVY FILLETS, CHOPPED

2 TABLESPOONS LEMON JUICE

FRESHLY GROUND BLACK PEPPER

ABOUT 2 TABLESPOONS OLIVE OIL

1 TABLESPOON FINELY CHOPPED TARRAGON OR FLAT-LEAVED PARSLEY

SERVES *6-8*

PREPARATION *10 minutes, plus chilling*

Calories per serving *67*
Total fat *High*
Saturated fat *Medium*
Protein *Low*
Carbohydrate *Low*
Cholesterol *Nil*
Vitamins *B12, E*
Minerals *Iron*

1 Place all the ingredients except oil and herbs in a food processor and blend until smooth.
2 With the machine still running, slowly add the olive oil. When 2 tablespoons has been added, taste and add a little more if necessary for a spreading consistency. Cover and chill.
3 Serve chilled, with the herbs sprinkled on top, and accompanied by warm toast.

Tyropitakia Lefteritsas

ROAST PEPPERS WITH ANCHOVY VINAIGRETTE

This is an improvisation of mine which became an instant success. The salty edge of the anchovies brings out the sweetness of the peppers. If you don't like strong tastes, however, reduce the number of anchovies in the dressing.

SERVES 4-6

PREPARATION *about 15 minutes*

COOKING *40 minutes, plus cooling*

Calories per serving *111*
Total fat *High*
Saturated fat *Low*
Protein *Low*
Carbohydrate *Low*
Cholesterol *Nil*
Vitamins *A, B₃, B₆, B₁₂, Folate, C, E*
Minerals *Iron, Potassium*

6 RED PEPPERS, OR A MIX OF RED AND YELLOW
FRESHLY GROUND BLACK PEPPER
2 TABLESPOONS CHOPPED OR WHOLE SMALL PURPLE BASIL LEAVES, TO GARNISH
1 LEMON CUT INTO WEDGES, TO SERVE

FOR THE ANCHOVY VINAIGRETTE:
4 TINNED OR BOTTLED ANCHOVIES, DRAINED AND COARSELY CHOPPED
1 GARLIC CLOVE, CHOPPED
JUICE OF 1 SMALL LEMON
2 TABLESPOONS OLIVE OIL

1 Preheat the oven to 190°C/375°F/gas 5 and cover a baking sheet with foil.
2 Place the peppers on the prepared baking sheet and bake for 40 minutes. Turn them over once halfway, if you remember.
3 Take the peppers out of the oven and, when they are cool enough to handle, peel them. Then halve them, trim off the tops and remove the seeds. Place the halves on a plate, outsides up, in a circle and set them aside. (This can be done the day before, but the peppers should then be covered with cling

film to prevent them drying out.)
4 Make the anchovy vinaigrette: place the anchovies, garlic and lemon juice in a blender or food processor and blend briefly. With the machine still running, add the oil in a steady stream and blend until well amalgamated into a runny velvety sauce.
5 Pour this dressing over the peppers, garnish with the basil leaves and season with some freshly ground black pepper. It can now wait for 1 or 2 hours before serving. Serve with lemon wedges.

Roast Peppers with Anchovy Vinaigrette

CROSTINI CON FUNGHI
Tuscan Mushroom Crostini

Probably the most famous part of Tuscan antipasti, crostini are slices of toasted bread layered with mouthwatering toppings. The most familiar are made with chicken livers, or black olives and anchovies.

40 G / 1½ OZ DRIED FUNGHI PORCINI

150 G / 5 OZ BUTTON MUSHROOMS OR CHESTNUT MUSHROOMS

2 TABLESPOONS OLIVE OIL

2 SHALLOTS, PEELED AND FINELY CHOPPED

2 GARLIC CLOVES, PEELED AND CRUSHED

1 TEASPOON BRANDY

½ TEASPOON DRIED OREGANO

1 FRENCH BAGUETTE, CUT INTO THIN SLICES

SALT AND FRESHLY GROUND BLACK PEPPER

SERVES *4*

PREPARATION *about 15 minutes, plus 20 minutes' soaking*

COOKING *about 25 minutes*

Calories per serving *357*
Total fat *High*
Saturated fat *Medium*
Protein *Low*
Carbohydrate *Low*
Cholesterol *Nil*
Vitamins *B₁, B₂, B₃, B₆, Folate, E*
Minerals *Calcium, Potassium, Iron, Zinc, Selenium*

1 Soak the dried mushrooms in a bowl of warm water for about 20 minutes. Lift them out carefully in order not to disturb the grit at the bottom of the bowl. Place them in another bowl and rinse a few times until the water appears clear of grit. Pat them dry and chop them coarsely. Pour the original soaking water through a muslin- or kitchen-paper-lined sieve and reserve.

2 Heat the oil in a wide-based pan and sauté the shallots until translucent. Add the garlic and then the reconstituted mushrooms with 150 ml / ¼ pt of the strained liquid, the brandy and the oregano. Cover and simmer gently for 15 minutes.

3 In the meantime, wipe the fresh mushrooms and chop them coarsely. Turn the heat up, add them to the pan and cook them briskly for 5-7 minutes uncovered, stirring occasionally until most of the liquid they produce has evaporated. Season.

4 When the contents of the pan are cooler, put them in a food processor and process very briefly – they should be chopped and not puréed. You can prepare the mixture up to this point in advance.

5 Toast the slices of French bread under a hot grill. Spread a generous layer of the mushroom mixture on top of each and serve immediately. The crostini can also be served warm or even cold.

BRUSCHETTA TOSCANA
Grilled Tuscan Bread with Olives

SERVES *4*

PREPARATION *about 20 minutes*

COOKING *about 5 minutes*

Bruschetta, *in its simplicity, is one of those culinary items at the heart of a culture. It originated in Rome – according to Marcella Hazan its name is derived from* bruscare, *which means 'to roast over coals' – and originally it was nothing more than fresh bread toasted and sprinkled with a thick green olive oil.*

**4 LARGE SLICES OF FRESH CRUSTY BREAD, ABOUT 1 CM/
½ IN THICK**

175 G / 6 OZ BLACK OLIVES

3 RIPE TOMATOES (ABOUT 225 G / 8 OZ)

2 TINNED SALTED ANCHOVIES

1 TABLESPOON LEMON JUICE

**3 GARLIC CLOVES, PEELED AND ROUGHLY CRUSHED
WITH THE FLAT OF A KNIFE**

2 TABLESPOONS OLIVE OIL

1 TABLESPOON FINELY CHOPPED BASIL LEAVES

FRESHLY GROUND BLACK PEPPER

Calories per serving *283*
Total fat *High*
Saturated fat *Low*
Protein *Low*
Carbohydrate *Low*
Cholesterol *Nil*
Vitamins *B₁, B₃, B₆, B₁₂,
Folate, E*
Minerals *Calcium, Iron,
Selenium, Potassium*

1 Blanch, peel, quarter and deseed the tomatoes. Set them aside. Stone the olives and place them with the anchovies and lemon juice in a food processor. Process rapidly for a few seconds until the mixture resembles breadcrumbs. Add the tomatoes and process rapidly for a few more seconds.

2 Grill the bread on both sides until crisp and golden and rub one side of each slice with the crushed garlic. Cut the slices in half to make them easier to handle. Dribble a little oil on the garlicky side and then add a thin – or thick, according to taste – layer of the olive and tomato mixture, some pepper and finally a little fresh basil. Serve immediately.

GRILLED HALOUMI ON A BED OF ROCKET

Cypriot haloumi cheese, with its elastic texture, is totally transformed when grilled. The real secret is to soak it in water for 30 minutes and then rinse it under cold running water to extract its saltiness. In the winter, when outdoor grilling is difficult, I use a heavy ridged cast-iron grill pan and the results are wonderful. The cheese should be served immediately, otherwise it becomes leathery.

**1 HALOUMI CHEESE (ABOUT 175 G / 6 OZ), SOAKED IN
COLD WATER FOR 30 MINUTES AND RINSED**

115 G / 4 OZ ROCKET, COARSELY CHOPPED

SEEDS OF 1 POMEGRANATE (SEE PAGE 19)

(OPTIONAL WHEN OUT OF SEASON)

1 TABLESPOON OLIVE OIL

1 TABLESPOON VEGETABLE OIL

FOR THE DRESSING:

2 TABLESPOONS OLIVE OIL

1 TABLESPOON BALSAMIC VINEGAR

SALT AND FRESHLY GROUND PEPPER

SERVES *4*

PREPARATION *about
15 minutes, plus
30 minutes' soaking*

COOKING *about
5 minutes*

Calories per serving *229*
Total fat *High*
Saturated fat *High*
Protein *Low*
Carbohydrate *Low*
Cholesterol *30 mg*
Vitamins *A, B₁₂, E*
Minerals *Calcium,
Potassium, Iron, Zinc*

1 Pat the cheese dry and slice it into 5-6 medium slices. Coat with olive oil and set them aside. Spread the rocket on a small platter and scatter pomegranate seeds all over.

2 Oil a cast-iron grill pan lightly with the vegetable oil and heat it until quite hot, but not smoking. Place the cheese slices on it and don't move them. Let them cook for a couple of minutes and then turn them over. Let them cook for 1-2 more minutes. Lift them and place them directly on the salad in a circle or fan shape.

3 While the cheese is cooking, beat the dressing ingredients lightly in a bowl and season to taste. Dribble the dressing over cheese and salad and serve immediately.

ANDALUSIAN GAZPACHO

'Reapers and agricultural labourers could never stand the sun's fire without this cooling acetous diet. This was the oxikratos *of the Greeks, the* posca, *potable food, meat and drinc,* potus et esca, *which formed part of the rations of the Roman soldiers…' wrote Richard Ford in his* Gatherings from Spain, *published in 1846. And he was right. In the midday heat of August, this makes a perfect lunch.*

2 SLICES OF STALE BREAD, CRUSTS REMOVED

900 G / 2 LB RIPE TOMATOES, PEELED AND CHOPPED

1 FRESH GREEN CHILLI, DESEEDED AND CHOPPED

7.5 CM / 3 IN LENGTH OF CUCUMBER, PEELED AND
COARSELY CHOPPED

2 GARLIC CLOVES, PEELED AND CRUSHED

½ GREEN OR RED SWEET PEPPER, DESEEDED AND
CHOPPED

2 TABLESPOONS OLIVE OIL

2 TABLESPOONS RED WINE VINEGAR

½ TEASPOON PAPRIKA

2 TABLESPOONS PARSLEY, CHOPPED

7-8 BASIL OR MINT LEAVES

SALT AND FRESHLY GROUND BLACK PEPPER

TO GARNISH:

LARGE HANDFUL OF BASIL, TORN INTO STRIPS

1 GREEN OR RED SWEET PEPPER, TRIMMED, DESEEDED
AND FINELY DICED

4 CM / 1½ IN CUCUMBER, PEELED AND FINELY DICED

3 TABLESPOONS FINELY DICED RED ONION

GARLIC CROUTONS

1 Soak the bread in water for 10 minutes, squeeze it a little and place it in a food processor or liquidizer with the remaining ingredients and 300 ml / ½ pt water. If the chilli is very hot, add only half. Process until smooth. Taste and adjust the seasoning. If you like a sharper taste add a little more vinegar.

2 Empty into a bowl, cover and chill for 2-3 hours or longer.

3 Before serving the soup, float 2-3 ice cubes in it to keep it chilled and, if needed, dilute it with a little more iced water. Serve the garnishes in separate small bowls and let people help themselves.

SERVES 6

PREPARATION *about 25 minutes, plus 10 minutes' soaking and 2-3 hours' chilling*

Calories per serving *130*
Total fat *Medium*
Saturated fat *Low*
Protein *Low*
Carbohydrate *Medium*
Cholesterol *Nil*
Vitamins A, B₁, B₃, B₆, Folate, E
Minerals *Potassium, Iron*

TURKISH COLD YOGHURT SOUP

The Turks are supposed to have brought yoghurt with them to Europe and they certainly display a preference for it. It is used in soups, served with poached eggs in cilbir, *spread over fried vegetables, used in salads with spinach or purslane, used to marinate kebabs, made into a cold drink called* ayran *and it features in* cacik, *the Turkish Yoghurt and Cucumber Salad (see page 40). This refreshing soup is identical to* cacik, *apart from the volume of ingredients. Proceed as for the* cacik *recipe, but add half the measured ingredients again and dilute with 150 ml / ¼ pint cold water, or a little more to taste. As well as the fresh mint, add also 2 tablespoons of finely chopped fresh dill. Serve chilled.*

Andalusian Gazpacho

SERVES 4-6

PREPARATION *15 minutes, plus chilling*

Calories per serving *76*
Total fat *High*
Saturated fat *Low*
Protein *High*
Carbohydrate *Low*
Cholesterol *3 mg*
Vitamins B₂, B₃
Minerals *Calcium, Iodine*

SOUPE AU PISTOU

This is not unlike Italian minestrone, *but it becomes intoxicating with the addition of the fragrant* pistou. *Its ingredients vary according to seasonal availability, so one can loosely improvise. A few years ago, for instance, I had a delicious version in Nice in the early summer, where everything used in the soup was green – fresh broad beans, peas, green beans and courgettes.*

Pistou *is like Pesto (page 33) without the pine nuts. It is mixed into the soup just before it is served and I offer an extra bowl of it along with a bowl of grated Parmesan cheese on the table.*

SERVES 6

PREPARATION *about 25 minutes, plus overnight soaking*

COOKING *about 50 minutes*

Calories per serving *300*
Total fat *High*
Saturated fat *High*
Protein *High*
Carbohydrate *Low*
Cholesterol *31 mg*
Vitamins *A, B group, E*
Minerals *Calcium, Iron, Zinc, Potassium*

[handwritten: Small White Navy bean]
85 G / 3 OZ ~~HARICOT~~ BEANS, SOAKED OVERNIGHT
2 TABLESPOONS OLIVE OIL
1 MEDIUM ONION, PEELED AND THINLY SLICED
2 LEEKS, FINELY CHOPPED
450 G / 1 LB TOMATOES, PEELED AND CHOPPED
2 SMALL POTATOES, DICED
[handwritten: Zucchini] 280 G / 10 OZ COURGETTES, DICED
2 SMALL CARROTS, DICED
150 G / 5 OZ GREEN BEANS, EACH CUT INTO 3-4 LENGTHS
1.3 LITRES / 2¼ PT HOT WATER
LARGE HANDFUL OF FLAT-LEAVED PARSLEY, CHOPPED

SMALL BUNCH OF CHERVIL, CHOPPED
50 G / 2 OZ SPAGHETTINI, BROKEN INTO SHORT PIECES
SALT AND FRESHLY GROUND BLACK PEPPER
115 G / 4 OZ FRESHLY GRATED PARMESAN TO SERVE

FOR THE PISTOU:
115 G / 4 OZ BASIL LEAVES
2 LARGE GARLIC CLOVES, PEELED AND CHOPPED
4 TABLESPOONS OLIVE OIL
50 G / 2 OZ PARMESAN CHEESE, FRESHLY GRATED
2 TABLESPOONS FRESHLY GRATED PECORINO SARDO OR ROMANO CHEESE

1 Rinse the haricot beans, cover with water and boil for about 30 minutes until soft. Strain and discard the liquid.

2 Heat the oil in a large saucepan, add the onion and sauté until glistening. Add the leeks and 1-2 minutes later, add the remaining vegetables including the boiled beans. Turn the vegetables with a spatula for 3-4 minutes to coat them in the oil.

3 Add the hot water with the herbs and seasoning to taste. Cover and simmer for 40 minutes.

4 While the soup is simmering, make the pistou: place all the ingredients apart from cheeses in a food processor and give it a quick burst. Stop and scrape everything down, then do it again. If the mixture appears too dry, add 1 tablespoon of water. When it has a creamy appearance, add the cheeses and give it one more rapid burst. Just before using it, dilute it a little by adding 2 tablespoonfuls of warm water.

5 About 20 minutes before the soup is to be served, bring it back to the boil. Add the pasta and simmer for 8-10 minutes. Remove the soup from the heat, mix in 3-4 tablespoons of pistou and serve. Offer the remaining pistou and the Parmesan in bowls.

ZUPPA DI CECI
Chickpea Soup

Chickpeas have a wonderfully nutty flavour which makes them the ideal warming winter staple. Each Mediterranean country has its own chickpea soup: in Italy it is zuppa di ceci, *in Greece it is* revythia soupa, *in Turkey there is* nohut çorbasi, *in Languedoc in France there is* soupe aux pois chiches. *The variations are endless and in Tuscany this particularly delicious soup is on every restaurant menu.*

Chickpeas are, of course, a wonderful store-cupboard ingredient, but they do have to be soaked in water overnight. A pressure cooker is ideal for cooking this dish.

SERVES *4*

PREPARATION *15-20 minutes, plus overnight soaking*

COOKING *about 1 hour if using a pressure cooker, otherwise about 2¼ hours*

Calories per serving *380*
Total fat *Medium*
Saturated fat *Low*
Protein *Medium*
Carbohydrate *Medium*
Cholesterol *Nil*
Vitamins *B₁, B₂, B₃, B₆, Folate, E*
Minerals *Calcium, Potassium, Iron, Zinc, Selenium*

225 G / 8 OZ CHICKPEAS, PICKED CLEAN AND SOAKED OVERNIGHT
3 TABLESPOONS OLIVE OIL
1 CELERY STALK WITH LEAVES, FINELY CHOPPED
SMALL SPRIG OF FRESH ROSEMARY, FINELY CHOPPED
6-7 FRESH SAGE LEAVES, FINELY CHOPPED, PLUS MORE WHOLE LEAVES FOR GARNISH (OPTIONAL)
4 GARLIC CLOVES, PEELED AND CRUSHED

1 SMALL TIN (200 G / 7 OZ) OF CHOPPED TOMATOES
JUICE OF ½ LEMON
SALT AND FRESHLY GROUND BLACK PEPPER

TO SERVE:
4 SMALL SLICES OF BREAD
2 GARLIC CLOVES, PEELED AND SLICED IN HALF LENGTHWISE

1 Rinse and drain the chickpeas. Place them in a pressure cooker, cover them with fresh water by at least 2.5 cm / 1 in and bring to the boil. Skim the white froth which rises to the surface until clear. Cover, weight and cook for about 15-20 minutes under full pressure. If using an ordinary saucepan, allow at least 1½ hours until the chickpeas are soft.

2 Drain, reserving the liquid. Take 2 cupfuls of chickpeas and liquidize them with 2 cups of the reserved liquid. Set this aside.

3 Heat the oil in the same saucepan and add the celery and herbs. A minute later add the garlic. As soon as the garlic becomes aromatic add the chopped tomatoes and sauté together for a few minutes. Add the remaining chickpeas and stir to coat them in the sauce for 3-4 minutes. Add at least 250 ml / ½ pt of the reserved liquid (if there is not enough, add a little water) with some seasoning. Cover and simmer for 20 minutes.

4 Stir in the liquidized chickpeas with their liquid, cover and simmer for 15 more minutes, stirring often as it may stick.

5 Add the lemon juice and, if necessary, dilute the soup to the desired consistency with a little more hot water. Adjust the seasoning.

6 Just before serving, toast the bread. While it is still hot, rub its surface with the garlic. Place a slice of bread in each soup bowl and pour the soup on top. Garnish with a few more sage leaves, if you wish.

Zuppa di Ceci

PASTA E FAGIOLI
Borlotti Bean and Pasta Soup

This is a great peasant Tuscan dish which is both substantial and soul-warming. There are countless versions of it, using all kinds of beans. I have had it in Venice with borlotti beans and I have made it with beautiful beans called pavone *– peacocks – that I bought in the Rialto market. These were large and plump and were adorned with all kinds of pink hues, like Venetian marbling. In addition to their pretty looks they had a very enticing taste.*

SERVES *4-6*

PREPARATION *about 20 minutes, plus overnight soaking*

COOKING *about 1¼ hours*

Calories per serving *376*
Total fat *Medium*
Saturated fat *Medium*
Protein *High*
Carbohydrate *Low*
Cholesterol *24 mg*
Vitamins *A, B group*
Minerals *Calcium, Potassium, Iron, Zinc*

280 G / 10 OZ BORLOTTI BEANS, PICKED CLEAN AND SOAKED OVERNIGHT
1 LARGE CARROT, DICED
3 TABLESPOONS OLIVE OIL
1 MEDIUM ONION, THINLY SLICED

50 G / 2 OZ PANCETTA, SLICED IN FINE STRIPS
85 G / 3 OZ SMALL TUBULAR PASTA
50 G /2 OZ FRESHLY GRATED PARMESAN CHEESE
SALT AND FRESHLY GROUND BLACK PEPPER

1 Rinse the beans, place them in a saucepan and cover with 1.3 litres / 2¼ pints water. Bring to the boil and skim. Add the carrot, cover and cook gently for about 40-50 minutes, until the beans are tender.

2 Take out half of the beans and mash them in a food processor with some of the cooking liquid. Empty them back into the pot and mix well.

3 Half an hour before it is to be served, finish the dish: heat the oil gently in a frying pan and sauté the onion until it starts to turn light golden. Turn up the heat a little, add the pancetta and sauté until crisp. Mix this into the beans, season to taste and bring back to the boil. The soup should be quite creamy but if too thick dilute with a little hot water.

4 Add the pasta and simmer gently for 6-7 minutes, stirring often as it may stick.

5 Off the heat, mix in half of the Parmesan and serve. Offer a bowl with the remaining Parmesan and some crusty bread.

KOTOPOULO SOUPA AVGOLEMONO
Chicken Soup with Egg-and-lemon Sauce

This very delicious soup could be served either as a first course or as a meal in itself for an informal occasion or a family lunch.

1 FREE-RANGE CHICKEN OR BOILING FOWL, WEIGHING ABOUT 1.5 KG / 3½ LB

1 ONION, PEELED AND SLICED IN HALF

2 CARROTS

2 CELERY STALKS, EACH TRIMMED AND SLICED INTO 3-4 PIECES

SMALL HANDFUL OF PARSLEY

3-4 BLACK PEPPERCORNS

SALT

50 G / 2 OZ SHORT-GRAIN RICE

1 QUANTITY EGG-AND-LEMON SAUCE (PAGE 36)

LEMON QUARTERS, TO SERVE

SERVES *6*

PREPARATION *10-15 minutes*

COOKING *about 1½ hours, plus cooling*

Calories per serving *150*
Total fat *Low*
Saturated fat *Low*
Protein *High*
Carbohydrate *Low*
Cholesterol *118 mg*
Vitamins *A, B group*
Minerals *Zinc, Potassium, Selenium, Iodine*

1 Rinse the chicken, place it in a large saucepan and cover with 1.75 litres / 3 pts water. Bring to the boil and skim until clear.
2 Add all the vegetables, the parsley, peppercorns and salt to taste. Cover and cook for about 1 hour, or 30 minutes longer if a boiling fowl is used. When the leg of the bird can be pulled easily away from the body, it is done. Take the chicken out, strain the broth and discard the vegetables.
3 Pull away the two breasts from the bird, skin them and discard the skin. Dice the meat. You can do the same with the leg meat if you want the soup to be more substantial, otherwise keep the legs – for a salad, perhaps.
4 Pour the broth back into the saucepan and add the breast meat. It can be prepared up to this stage well in advance, even the day before.
5 About a quarter of an hour before the soup is to be served, bring it back to the boil and add the rice. Cover and cook for about 8 minutes. Let it cool off the heat for 5 minutes.
6 Make the sauce while the soup is cooling: Add a ladleful of chicken broth to the egg mixture slowly and beat together for 1 minute and then add another ladleful and beat. By now the sauce will be warm, so you can pour it slowly into the soup, off the heat, and stir vigorously to mix.
7 Warm the soup up over a very, very gentle heat – otherwise the eggs may cook, although the cornflour will safeguard against that.
8 Serve immediately, with a plate of lemon quarters on the table and fresh bread.

Pasta, Rice & Grains

CHARD CANNELLONI WITH PINE NUTS

When I first went to Rome in 1962 the two dishes which impressed me most were spaghetti alle vongole and cannelloni. I remember buying squares of fresh pasta and taking them back home to my mother in Athens in order to re-create cannelloni. For this vegetarian version I use Swiss chard – which has a sweeter taste than spinach, and an aroma which reminds me of the open fields – a number of different cheeses and pine nuts or occasionally coarsely chopped walnuts for a difference in texture.

SERVES 6

PREPARATION
40 minutes

COOKING
about 1 hour

Calories per serving *718*
Total fat *High*
Saturated fat *High*
Protein *Medium*
Carbohydrate *Low*
Cholesterol *157 mg*
Vitamins *A, B group, C, E*
Minerals *Calcium, Potassium, Iron, Zinc, Selenium, Iodine*

24 QUICK-COOK CANNELLONI TUBES
(ABOUT 350 G / 12 OZ)
1 KG / 2¼ LB SWISS CHARD, OR 900 G / 2 LB FRESH
SPINACH, OR 250 G / 9 OZ FROZEN LEAF SPINACH,
DEFROSTED
85 G / 3 OZ PINE NUTS, TOASTED LIGHTLY
175 G / 6 OZ FRESH RICOTTA CHEESE
2 TABLESPOONS OLIVE OIL

1 MEDIUM ONION, FINELY CHOPPED
LARGE HANDFUL OF BASIL, LEAVES AND STALKS,
CHOPPED
1 EGG
85 G / 3 OZ FRESHLY GRATED PARMESAN CHEESE
85 G / 3 OZ FRESHLY GRATED PECORINO CHEESE
1 LITRE / 1¾ PINTS BÉCHAMEL SAUCE (PAGE 36)
PEPPER

1 If using chard or larger older spinach leaves, trim off and discard the thick stalks. Fill the sink with water and soak the leaves in this for 10 minutes in order to dislodge any grit. Lift the leaves out by hand and repeat the process until the water appears clear. Put the leaves in a large saucepan with a little salt, cover and cook gently for 10-15 minutes, stirring occasionally and making sure they don't dry out. Drain through a colander and gently squeeze out excess moisture (carefully, as it will still be quite hot). Chop the leaves coarsely. If using defrosted frozen spinach, just squeeze its moisture out and chop it.
2 Preheat the oven 180°C/350°F/gas 4 and lightly oil one large or two medium-sized ovenproof dishes which can be brought from the oven straight to the table. Heat the remaining oil gently in a frying pan and sauté

the onion until glistening. Add the chopped chard or spinach leaves and the basil and sauté together for 3-4 minutes. Let this cool a little.
3 Beat the egg lightly in a large bowl, add the ricotta and, using a fork, mix it with the egg. Add two-thirds of the Parmesan and all of the Pecorino, the sautéed leaves, the pine nuts and 3 tablespoons of the béchamel. The stuffing should be of a thick creamy consistency, but not solid. Season to taste with pepper.
4 Stuff the cannelloni with the filling, using a small spoon or knife and pushing the stuffing down with a chopstick or a skewer. Place the stuffed cannelloni tightly together in a single layer in the prepared dish(es) and spread the remaining béchamel sauce evenly over them. Sprinkle the top with the remaining Parmesan and bake for 40-45 minutes, until the top is golden and the cannelloni properly cooked.

Chard Cannelloni with Pine Nuts

PENNE CON SALSA CRUDA
Penne with Raw Tomato Sauce

This very refreshing and light dish is one to be made at the height of the summer when the weather is hot and tomatoes are sugary. Our friend Guido Jesurum introduced us to it back in 1972, in his lovely house overlooking Mount Etna on the Aeolian island of Salina.

400 G / **14** OZ PENNE RIGATE OR OTHER PASTA
1 TABLESPOON OLIVE OIL
SALT AND FRESHLY GROUND BLACK PEPPER
FRESHLY GRATED **P**ARMESAN CHEESE, TO SERVE

FOR THE **S**ALSA **C**RUDA:

675 G / **1½** LB LARGE RIPE TOMATOES
2 GARLIC CLOVES, PEELED AND CRUSHED
2 TABLESPOONS OLIVE OIL
1 TABLESPOON GOOD-QUALITY CAPERS, RINSED
LARGE HANDFUL OF BASIL, SHREDDED BY HAND

SERVES *4*

PREPARATION *about 10 minutes*

COOKING *10-15 minutes, depending on the pasta*

Calories per serving *849*
Total fat *Low*
Saturated fat *Low*
Protein *Low*
Carbohydrate *High*
Cholesterol *10 mg*
Vitamins *A, B group, C, E*
Minerals *Calcium, Potassium, Iron, Zinc, Selenium*

1 First prepare the tomatoes for the sauce: peel them and, holding them from the stem end, grate them coarsely. Alternatively, peel them, trim off their stalks and place them in a food processor and process rapidly to achieve a coarse consistency. Put the grated or processed tomatoes in a bowl, cover and keep them refrigerated if they are not to be used immediately.

2 Cook the pasta: bring a large pan of lightly salted water to the boil, add ½ tablespoon of the olive oil and cook the pasta in it until just al dente – tender but still firm. Drain and mix with the remaining oil.

3 Just before the dish is to be served, mix the tomatoes with the remaining sauce ingredients and season with pepper. Pour over the pasta and toss.

4 Serve immediately, with a bowl of grated Parmesan served separately.

PENNE WITH SUN-DRIED TOMATOES AND MOZZARELLA

This easy dish is quite delicious, with the Mozzarella cubes mellowing the robustness of the sun-dried tomatoes. The sauce has to be prepared very rapidly, 5-7 minutes in total, and must be consumed immediately, before the Mozzarella becomes leathery. Other pasta shapes, such as fusilli, farfalle or orecchiette, can be used instead of the penne.

400 G / 14 OZ PENNE
6-8 SUN-DRIED TOMATO HALVES IN OIL, CHOPPED
150 G / 5 OZ BUFFALO MOZZARELLA CHEESE, CUT INTO 2 CM / ¾ IN DICE
3 TABLESPOONS OLIVE OIL
3 GARLIC CLOVES, PEELED AND CRUSHED

350 G / 12 OZ CHERRY TOMATOES
4 LARGE SPRIGS OF FRESH BASIL (INCLUDING STEMS), TORN BY HAND
SALT AND FRESHLY GROUND BLACK PEPPER
FRESHLY GRATED PARMESAN CHEESE, TO SERVE

1 Boil the pasta in plenty of lightly salted water until just al dente. Drain and keep warm.

2 Heat the oil in the same saucepan, and add the sun-dried tomatoes and garlic. As soon as the garlic becomes aromatic, add the whole cherry tomatoes and roll them around with a wooden spatula over gentle heat for just 1 minute to coat them in the oil. The cherry tomatoes should still be intact.

3 Add the pasta, the basil and a generous sprinkling of pepper. Toss for 1-2 minutes to mix with the tomatoes and garlic. Add the Mozzarella, mix it in quickly and allow it just to warm through. Remove the pan from the heat before the cheese starts to melt and become sticky. Serve immediately, with freshly grated Parmesan.

SERVES *4 as a main course, or 6 as a first course*

PREPARATION
10 minutes

COOKING
15-20 minutes, depending on the pasta

Calories per serving *641*
Total fat *Medium*
Saturated fat *Medium*
Protein *Low*
Carbohydrate *Low*
Cholesterol *23 mg*
Vitamins *A, B group, C, E*
Minerals *Calcium, Potassium, Iron, Zinc, Selenium*

Overleaf, left to right: Conchiglie with Seafood (page 70),
Penne with Sun-Dried Tomatoes and Mozzarella, Spaghetti alle Vongole (page 71)

SPAGHETTI CON LE ACCIUGHE
Spaghetti with Anchovy and Caper Sauce

This is our family's favourite sauce when we are in our house in the Aegean island of Alonnisos in the summer. Although the sauce has a strong piquant taste, once it has coated the pasta it loses its forcefulness and becomes quite tame. It is quick and easy to prepare and everyone loves it.

SERVES *4*

PREPARATION *10 minutes*

COOKING *about 30 minutes*

Calories per serving *468*
Total fat *Low*
Saturated fat *Low*
Protein *Low*
Carbohydrate *High*
Cholesterol *Nil*
Vitamins *B group, C*
Minerals *Iron, Zinc, Potassium*

400 G / 14 OZ SPAGHETTI OR LINGUINE

50 G / 2 OZ TIN OF ANCHOVIES IN OIL, DRAINED AND CHOPPED

1½ TABLESPOONS CAPERS, RINSED AND DRAINED

2-3 TABLESPOONS OLIVE OIL

2 LARGE ONIONS, ABOUT 350 G / 12 OZ, PEELED AND THINLY SLICED

1-2 GREEN CHILLIES, DESEEDED AND FINELY CHOPPED

3 GARLIC CLOVES, PEELED AND CRUSHED

10 BLACK OLIVES

2 TABLESPOONS FINELY CHOPPED PARSLEY

FRESHLY GROUND BLACK PEPPER

1 Heat the oil gently in a medium-sized saucepan and add the onions. Stir to coat them in the oil and cook until they become translucent, about 4-5 minutes.

2 Add the chilli(es) and stir together for 1-2 minutes to allow them to release their oils and aroma. Then immediately stir in the garlic and, as soon as its aroma rises – almost immediately – add 150 ml / ¼ pt water and simmer gently for 10 minutes so that the onions get cooked and become more digestible.

3 Add the anchovies, capers, olives, parsley and pepper and simmer for 5 more minutes.

4 While the sauce is being prepared, cook the pasta in a large pan of lightly salted boiling water, drain and keep some of the pasta water aside. Return the pasta to the pan, add the anchovy sauce and 2 tablespoons of the reserved pasta water. Toss gently to mix everything and coat the pasta in the sauce.

CONCHIGLIE WITH SEAFOOD

Conchiglie – sea shells – fits thematically with seafood, but any pasta with cavities, such as fusilli, penne or the Apulian orecchiette – little ears – will do. Mussels are indispensable to the dish as they add an unparalleled flavour of the sea. (See previous pages.)

SERVES *4 as a main course, or 6 as a first course*

PREPARATION *20-25 minutes*

COOKING *40-45 minutes, depending on the pasta*

400 G / 14 OZ CONCHIGLIE

675 G / 1½ LB FRESH MUSSELS, PREPARED AS ON PAGE 93

500 G / 1 LB 2 OZ SQUID, PREPARED AS ON PAGE 75

175 G / 6 OZ COOKED PEELED PRAWNS

150 ML / ¼ PINT WHITE WINE

3 TABLESPOONS OLIVE OIL

1 LARGE ONION, FINELY CHOPPED

3 GARLIC CLOVES, PEELED AND CHOPPED

2-3 SPRIGS OF FRESH OREGANO, CHOPPED

3-4 SPRIGS OF BASIL, TORN BY HAND

SALT AND FRESHLY GROUND BLACK PEPPER

1 Place the mussels in a large saucepan with the wine. Cover and boil briskly for 5 minutes or until they open, shaking the pan vigorously from time to time. Let them cool a little.

2 Using a slotted spoon, lift the mussels out and transfer to a bowl. Let the liquid settle so that grit sinks. Discard any which remain closed. Take most out of their shells and place them in another bowl, but leave a few in their shells for visual effect. To keep the mussels moist, strain their liquor over them through a fine sieve lined with kitchen paper.

3 The squid bodies should be kept intact, rinsed inside and out and then sliced into thin rings; divide the tentacles into 3-4 pieces.

4 Heat the oil gently in a large pan and sauté the onion until lightly golden. Add the garlic. When it is aromatic, add the squid and sauté for 10-15 minutes, until all moisture evaporates.

5 Add most of the strained mussel liquid, the oregano and seasoning. Cover and cook gently for 15-20 minutes, until the squid is just tender. If needed, add a little hot water. Add the prawns and cook for 2-3 minutes. Mix in the mussels and basil and remove from heat.

6 While the squid is cooking, cook the pasta in plenty of boiling water until al dente. Drain and mix into the seafood mixture. Serve.

Calories per serving *526*
Total fat *Low*
Saturated fat *Low*
Protein *High*
Carbohydrate *Low*
Cholesterol *345 mg*
Vitamins *B group, E*
Minerals *Calcium, Potassium, Iodine, Selenium, Iron, Zinc*

SPAGHETTI ALLE VONGOLE
Spaghetti with Clams and Garlic

Small white Mediterranean clams appear occasionally at fishmongers and are cheap (See pages 68-9).

285 G / 10 OZ SPAGHETTI
1.5 KG / 2½ LB CLAMS
2-3 GARLIC CLOVES, PEELED AND CRUSHED
3 TABLESPOONS GOOD OLIVE OIL

3 SPRING ONIONS, THINLY SLICED
3 TABLESPOONS FINELY CHOPPED PARSLEY
3 TABLESPOONS FINELY CHOPPED FRESH DILL
SALT AND FRESHLY GROUND BLACK PEPPER

SERVES *2 as main course, or 4 as a first course*

PREPARATION *about 20 minutes*

COOKING *about 15 minutes*

1 Place the clams in a large bowl of cold water and let their grit sink. Lift out and repeat the process until water is perfectly clear. Discard any that remain open after they are tapped.

2 Heat the oil in a large frying pan and sauté the spring onions gently in it without allowing them to brown. Add the garlic and parsley and sauté briefly until aromatic.

3 Turn the heat up, add the clams and stir continuously for 2-3 minutes to coat them in the oil. Remove the pan from heat and let the clams stand briefly until slightly cooler.

4 Working quickly, pick half the clams out of their shells and discard the shells. (Discard any that may not have opened.)

5 While the clams are cooking, boil the spaghetti in plenty of lightly salted water for about 8 minutes, making sure it is not overcooked. Drain, reserving a cup of liquid.

6 Heat the clams up again if necessary, stirring continuously. Add some pepper, the dill, 2-3 tablespoons of the reserved cooking liquid and the pasta. Mix well over gentle heat for a few seconds to coat the pasta and serve.

Calories per serving *450*
Total fat *Low*
Saturated fat *Low*
Protein *High*
Carbohydrate *High*
Cholesterol *112 mg*
Vitamins *A, B group*
Minerals *Calcium, Potassium, Iron, Zinc, Iodine*

ASPARAGUS RISOTTO

This is a risotto with a very refined taste and elegant looks, making it perfect for a summer lunch or an al fresco dinner. It is best to make the stock beforehand, so the dish is not too laborious on the day. Allow about 85 g / 3 oz arborio, carnaroli or vialone nano rice per person. Remember that a risotto has to be cooked and consumed immediately, while it is still smooth and creamy. A crisp, green salad and fresh bread are the perfect accompaniment to the dish.

SERVES *4-5*

PREPARATION *about 20 minutes*

COOKING *40-45 minutes*

Calories per serving *454*
Total fat *Low*
Saturated fat *Medium*
Protein *Low*
Carbohydrate *High*
Cholesterol *22 mg*
Vitamins *A, B group, C, E*
Minerals *Calcium, Potassium, Iron, Zinc, Selenium, Iodine*

400 G / 14 OZ ASPARAGUS, TRIMMED OF HARD STEMS
400 G / 14 OZ RISOTTO RICE
3 TABLESPOONS SINGLE CREAM
LARGE HANDFUL OF BASIL LEAVES, ROUGHLY TORN
3 TABLESPOONS OLIVE OIL
1 MEDIUM ONION, PEELED AND FINELY CHOPPED

4-5 SPRING ONIONS, COARSELY CHOPPED
150 ML / ¼ PINT DRY WHITE WINE
1.2 LITRES / 2 PINTS HOT CHICKEN OR BEEF STOCK, WITH FAT REMOVED
85 G / 3 OZ GRATED PARMESAN CHEESE
SALT AND FRESHLY GROUND BLACK PEPPER

1 Cut the asparagus tips off and set aside. Cut each stalk into two and cook in plenty of lightly salted boiling water for 2 minutes. Remove from the pan with a slotted spoon and drain. Next drop the tips in the boiling water and boil very briefly, for 30 seconds only. Take out of the pan and drain separately.
2 Place just over half of the stalk pieces in a liquidizer with the cream, a few basil leaves and stems, and 2-3 tablespoons of the asparagus cooking liquid. Liquidize to a light green velvety sauce and set aside. Chop the remaining stalk pieces into thin rounds.
3 Heat the oil in a heavy wide-based pan and sauté the onion and spring onions in it until just wilted. Add the rice gradually, stirring over a gentle heat until well coated in the oil. Add the wine and, once absorbed, start adding ladlefuls of the hot stock and 150 ml / ¼ pt of the asparagus cooking liquid. Keep stirring to prevent the rice from sticking.

4 After about 25 minutes – when the rice has doubled its volume, is losing its chalky colour and is becoming soft – season to taste and add the liquidized asparagus. Stir it gently into the risotto, which will turn a lovely pale green colour. Simmer for 10 more minutes. Keep tasting the rice at this stage in order to catch it at the desired moment. It should be soft outside but firm in the middle. It should also have a very creamy appearance, so add more liquid if necessary.
5 Once the risotto is ready, add the remaining basil, half of the Parmesan, the asparagus stalk segments and half of the tips. Mix gently, cover and turn the heat off. It can now wait for 5 minutes but no more.
6 Empty on to a warm platter, scatter the remaining asparagus over the top, garnish with a few more basil leaves if you wish and serve with a bowl of the remaining cheese.

Asparagus Risotto

LINGUINE CON PEPERONI ARROSTITI
Linguine with Roast Pepper Sauce

Inspired by a pasta dish with peperonade *(sautéed pepper strips) served by my friend Henriette Valvini, this fresh approach to pasta uses a light sauce which, nevertheless, has a sophisticated taste. This treatment also suits other types of pastas, such as rigatoni, penne or conchiglie.*

For a rather rich addition, roast a respectable amount of whole garlic cloves – about 15 – wrapped in foil in the oven with the peppers for 40 minutes, and then squeeze the delicious roast garlic pulp out of each clove over the pasta.

450 G / 1 LB LINGUINE

6 RED (OR A MIXTURE OF RED AND YELLOW) SWEET PEPPERS, RINSED AND DRIED

2 TABLESPOONS OLIVE OIL

3 GARLIC CLOVES, FINELY CHOPPED

2 TABLESPOONS SINGLE CREAM OR LOW-FAT FROMAGE FRAIS

4-5 LARGE SPRIGS OF FRESH BASIL, TORN BY HAND

SALT AND FRESHLY GROUND BLACK PEPPER

50 G / 2 OZ PECORINO ROMANO OR PARMESAN CHEESE, FRESHLY GRATED, TO SERVE

SERVES *4-5*

PREPARATION *10-15 minutes*

COOKING *45-50 minutes*

Calories per serving *464*

Total fat *Low*

Saturated fat *Low*

Protein *Low*

Carbohydrate *Low*

Cholesterol *13 mg*

Vitamins *A, B group, C, E*

Minerals *Calcium, Potassium, Iron, Zinc, Selenium*

1 Preheat the oven to 190°C/375°F/gas 5 and line a baking sheet with foil. Place the peppers on the prepared baking sheet, leaving a little space between them, and roast for 30-35 minutes, turning them over once halfway.

2 Take the peppers out of the oven, let them cool a little and then peel them, discarding tops, white pith and seeds as you go. Slice the pepper flesh in thin strips and set aside.

3 Heat the oil in a large frying pan and sauté the garlic in it until aromatic. Add the peppers and sauté for 3-4 minutes to coat them in the oil and garlic. Sprinkle in some seasoning and remove from the heat.

4 Place half of the pepper mixture in a food processor, add the cream or fromage frais and process until smooth.

5 Towards the end of the pepper cooking time, bring a large saucepan with plenty of water to the boil. Add a little salt and cook the pasta until just al dente. Drain, reserving a cupful of the liquid, and place the pasta back in the saucepan.

6 Dilute the smooth pepper sauce with 3 tablespoons of the cooking liquid and pour the light pink sauce over the pasta.

7 Heat up the remaining peppers in the frying pan, add the basil and toss around for a few seconds only until it looks a little wilted. Empty the contents of the pan into the pasta and toss with a fork to coat all the strands with the sauce. If it appears too dry, add a little more of the pasta liquid. If you have opted for the whole roast cloves of garlic, this is the moment to add in their pulp, simply squeezing each clove.

8 Serve immediately, with a bowl of cheese on the table.

RISOTTO NERO
Venetian Black Squid Risotto

The black squid risotto is a landmark of Venetian cuisine and the addition of the ink makes the risotto quite sweet. If you don't like it black, however, discard the ink sacs. The squid casserole should be prepared in advance. The rice takes about 35-40 minutes and it can be cooked while people are having their first course. It must then be consumed immediately. An absolute must for its taste is the fish stock, which can be made from bones and heads.

800 G / 1¾ LB LARGE SQUID

2 TABLESPOONS OLIVE OIL

2 MEDIUM ONIONS, SLICED

1 GLASS OF DRY WHITE WINE

SALT AND FRESHLY GROUND BLACK PEPPER

FOR THE RISOTTO:

450 G / 1 LB ARBORIO OR VIALONE

NANO RICE

3-4 SHALLOTS, THINLY SLICED

4 SPRING ONIONS, THICKLY SLICED

2 TABLESPOONS OLIVE OIL

1 GLASS OF DRY WHITE WINE

1.3 LITRES / 2¼ PINTS FISH STOCK (PAGE 37)

2-3 TABLESPOONS CHOPPED FRESH DILL

SERVES *6*

PREPARATION *20 minutes*

COOKING *about 1½ hours*

Calories per serving *513*
Total fat *Low*
Saturated fat *Low*
Protein *High*
Carbohydrate *Medium*
Cholesterol *300 mg*
Vitamins *B group, E*
Minerals *Potassium, Iron, Zinc, Selenium, Iodine*

1 First prepare the squid by pulling heads away from bodies. Slice the bodies open and empty them of all the innards. Dislodge and set aside the small elongated ink sacs (they look silver). Slice off and discard the upper part of each head, keeping the tentacles with a thin collar-like stripe on top. Rinse thoroughly and drain. Slice everything in long thin strips.
2 Heat the oil in a medium saucepan and sauté the onions until they start to turn light golden. Add the prepared squid strips, turn up the heat and sauté for about 10 minutes, turning continuously, until all the liquid evaporates and the squid starts to stick.
3 Add the wine with an equal quantity of water and season. Cover and cook gently for 15-20 minutes, until the squid is tender. Add the ink sacs and cook for 5 more minutes.

4 For the risotto you need a large wide-based saucepan or sauté pan. Fry the shallots and spring onions in the olive oil until they glisten. Add the rice gradually and stir over a gentle heat until it is coated in the oil. Add the wine and, when it is all absorbed, start adding the hot fish stock gradually, a ladleful at a time, stirring until it is absorbed.
5 After half an hour, add the squid and more seasoning and mix well. Continue adding the fish stock. About 5 minutes later, start tasting grains of rice. You may not need all the stock, as the rice must be caught at the precise moment when it is tender but its middle still feels a little hard. It must not be overcooked as it becomes like a sticky ball.
6 Remove the pan from the heat, mix in the fresh herbs and serve immediately.

BURANI
A Princely Pilaff

Burani *was originally a family of aubergine dishes cooked for Princess Buran's wedding to the powerful Caliph al-Mamoun, son of Harun al-Rashid, in ninth-century Baghdad. Her real name was Khadijah, but she was better known under the pet name of Buran, after a Persian princess of the seventh century. There are still dishes called* braniya *in both Algeria and Morocco, which centre round aubergines and meat. How could this lead to present day* burani *or* borani *or, in fact, the Indian* biryani*, which are all glorified pilaffs? Such are the mysteries of culinary evolution! I suspect that the dish was transformed with the addition of grain in Turkey. Haven't the Ottomans been great lovers of rice and aren't Turkish pilaffs monumental and referred to by all sorts of literature, throughout the ages?*

I was introduced to burani *as a child by our next-door neighbours in Athens, a family of refugees from Smyrna who had fled the catastrophic war of 1922. The name of the dish did not make any sense to me until some years ago, when I read an article by Charles Perry in the* Journal of Gastronomy. *It was such a splendid story that I love recounting it. It is my husband who has adopted* burani *now and he regularly makes it in the summer on the island when we have mounds of sugary tomatoes.*

We serve it with plain yoghurt and a plate of Feta or fresh goats' cheese and a large green salad.

---

400 G / 14 OZ LONG-GRAIN RICE

1 LARGE ONION, PEELED AND FINELY CHOPPED

3 TABLESPOONS OLIVE OIL

1 LARGE RED SWEET PEPPER, DESEEDED AND THINLY SLICED

4 GARLIC CLOVES, FINELY CHOPPED

1.35 KG / 3 LB RIPE TOMATOES, PEELED AND CHOPPED

1 TABLESPOON TOMATO PASTE

450 ML / ¾ PINT WATER

LARGE PINCH OF GROUND ALLSPICE

1 SMALL CINNAMON STICK OR A PINCH OF CINNAMON

½ TEASPOON SUGAR

4 TABLESPOONS FINELY CHOPPED PARSLEY, PLUS MORE PARSLEY SPRIGS TO GARNISH (OPTIONAL)

2 TABLESPOONS FINELY CHOPPED FRESH DILL

SALT AND FRESHLY GROUND BLACK PEPPER

SERVES *4-5*

PREPARATION *20 minutes*

COOKING *35-40 minutes*

Calories per serving *438*

Total fat *Low*

Saturated fat *Low*

Protein *Low*

Carbohydrate *High*

Cholesterol *Nil*

Vitamins *A, B₁, B₃, B₆, Folate, C, E*

Minerals *Potassium, Iron, Zinc, Iodine*

---

1 Sauté the onion in the hot oil until light golden. Add the red pepper and, 2 minutes later, the garlic. Sauté everything together for a minute, without allowing it to brown.

2 Add the rest of the ingredients, apart from rice and the herbs, and simmer for 10 minutes until the sauce is thicker.

3 Mix in the rice and parsley. Season to taste, cover and cook gently until the water has been absorbed, approximately 15-20 minutes. Test the rice after 15 minutes and, if needed in the meantime, add a little hot water.

4 When the rice is just tender, mix in the dill and remove from heat. The dish should be quite moist and the rice not overcooked. Garnish with more parsley if you wish.

Burani

POLENTA

A few years ago, one of the many reasons I would look forward to going to Venice was to have polenta, but now instant versions have brought it to our door. Polenta is made with maize or cornmeal flour. Once cooked, it may be eaten as it is or it can be prepared as below. You only need small portions of the polenta and a lot of sauce. Serve it with the black squid on page 75 or with a thick tomato sauce (see page 32).

SERVES 4-6

PREPARATION 10 minutes

COOKING 10-15 minutes, plus cooling

Calories per serving *193*
Total fat *Medium*
Saturated fat *High*
Protein *Low*
Carbohydrate *Low*
Cholesterol *14 mg*
Vitamins *B₃*
Minerals *Iron, Zinc*

175 G / **6** OZ INSTANT POLENTA
½ TEASPOON SALT

25 G / 1 OZ BUTTER
1 TABLESPOON OLIVE OIL

1 Bring 850 ml / 1½ pt water to the boil in a large heavy pan and add the salt. Turn the heat down a little and start adding the polenta in a thin but steady stream, stirring. Once it has all been added and it starts to bubble, turn the heat down and simmer for 3-4 minutes, continuing to stir or it will stick.
2 Turn the heat off, mix in the butter and

empty into an oiled quiche dish or other heatproof dish. Let stand for a few hours.
3 Just before serving, preheat a hot grill, oil the top of the polenta and grill for a few minutes, until the top becomes crisp and light golden. Cut it into thin slices and serve. Alternatively, cut the polenta into thicker wedges, oil these and grill for 2 minutes on each side.

SAFFRON RICE WITH ORANGE AND NUTS

SERVES 4

PREPARATION 20-30 minutes

COOKING 10-15 minutes

Calories per serving *346*
Total fat *Medium*
Saturated fat *Low*
Protein *Low*
Carbohydrate *High*
Cholesterol *Nil*
Vitamins *B₁, B₂, B₃, B₆, Folate, C, E*
Minerals *Potassium, Zinc, Iron*

175 G / **6** OZ LONG-GRAIN RICE, RINSED
2 LARGE PINCHES OF SAFFRON THREADS, CRUSHED
1 ORANGE, PEELED AND CUT INTO THIN DISCS
2 TABLESPOONS PINE NUTS, LIGHTLY TOASTED
GRATED ZEST AND JUICE OF 1 UNCOATED ORANGE
2 TABLESPOONS SHELLED PISTACHIO NUTS, LIGHTLY TOASTED AND CHOPPED
115 G / 4 OZ DRIED APRICOTS, COARSELY CHOPPED

2 TABLESPOONS SULTANAS OR RAISINS, RINSED
3 TABLESPOONS FINELY CHOPPED FRESH MINT
SALT

FOR THE VINAIGRETTE:
2 TABLESPOONS SHERRY VINEGAR
3 TABLESPOONS HAZELNUT OIL
1 TEASPOON SUNFLOWER OIL

1 Bring a saucepan of lightly salted water to the boil, add the rice and saffron, cover and cook until the rice is tender but still quite firm. Drain and place the rice in a bowl.
2 Make the vinaigrette: whisk the vinegar together with the juice from the orange.

Season with salt, add the oils and whisk again. Then pour over the rice while it is still warm.
3 Add the remaining ingredients and toss together to mix everything properly. Adjust the seasoning with some more salt, if necessary. Serve at room temperature.

Polenta, with black squid

SAFFRON PENNE SALAD WITH TIGER PRAWNS

Pasta salads can make delicious impromptu meals and one can improvise with available ingredients. There are two good rules for successful pasta salads. First, make sure that the pasta is slightly undercooked, so that it will hold its shape and texture when dressed. The second rule is to dress it while it is still hot and before it dries up and becomes sticky. Of course, a delicious vinaigrette is the most important ingredient. In the spring and early summer, one can have pasta with seasonal vegetables such as shelled broad beans and peas or asparagus and liven it up with fresh herbs. Alternatively, you can add grilled or roast vegetables, such as aubergines, courgettes and peppers. Add some finely chopped fresh herbs and be bold with the vinaigrette. It could have a North African flavour if you season it with cumin, ginger and garlic, or a tablespoon of harissa; you can use an olive or walnut oil with any of a number of vinegars, from Spanish sherry to Italian balsamic or a good French wine vinegar. It could even be a mixture of fromage frais or yoghurt with olive oil and garlic ... experiment!

If you were feeling extravagant you could add 4-6 scallops with the prawns (slice them in thin discs first) or some cooked and shelled mussels at the end.

SERVES *6 as a first course, or 4 as a main course*

PREPARATION *10 minutes*

COOKING *10-15 minutes, depending on the pasta*

Calories per serving *304*
Total fat *Low*
Saturated fat *Low*
Protein *High*
Carbohydrate *Medium*
Cholesterol *126 mg*
Vitamins *B group*
Minerals *Potassium, Iron, Zinc, Selenium, Iodine*

275 G / 10 OZ PENNE

2 LARGE PINCHES OF SAFFRON THREADS, CRUMBLED

225 G / 8 OZ SHELLED COOKED TIGER PRAWNS

2 TABLESPOONS OLIVE OIL

2 GARLIC CLOVES, PEELED AND THINLY SLICED

140 G / 5 OZ BUTTON MUSHROOMS

2 TABLESPOONS FINELY CHOPPED CHIVES

2-3 SPRIGS OF FRESH BASIL, TORN BY HAND

FOR THE VINAIGRETTE:

1½ TABLESPOONS BALSAMIC VINEGAR

1 GARLIC CLOVE, PEELED AND CRUSHED

2 TABLESPOONS OLIVE OIL

SALT AND FRESHLY GROUND BLACK PEPPER

1 Bring plenty of lightly salted water to the boil in a large saucepan, add the saffron and then the pasta. Cook until the pasta is just al dente — tender but still firm. Drain the pasta and turn it into a large bowl.

2 In the meantime, in a heavy-based or non-stick frying pan, heat the oil and add the prawns and the garlic. Sauté these for 2 minutes, turn the heat up and add the mushrooms, tossing everything together and turning them over brisk heat for about 3 minutes. Season to taste, add the chives and the basil and sauté for 1 more minute, until the herbs look just wilted. Add this to the pasta in the bowl and mix together.

3 Whisk the vinegar, seasoning and garlic for the vinaigrette together and then add the oil and whisk until well amalgamated. Adjust the seasoning. It should be quite sharp.

4 Add the vinaigrette to the pasta and toss gently to coat everything. It can now wait, covered with film, if necessary. It can be served warm or at room temperature or, in the summer, slightly chilled.

BULGURI PILAFI
Cracked Wheat and Vermicelli Pilaff

This earthy dish from the island of Cyprus is quick and easy to prepare and it makes a delicious partner to grilled poultry and meat, or casseroles of meat or vegetables. It goes well with plain yoghurt or a yoghurt sauce such as Sarimsakli Yoghurt (page 33). It is the ideal standby dish, as the basic ingredients can happily live in the store cupboard for a long time.

250 G / 9 OZ COARSE (IDEALLY NOT FINE) BULGAR, PICKED CLEAN

50 G / 2 OZ VERMICELLI

3 TABLESPOONS OLIVE OIL

1 ONION, THINLY SLICED

350 ML / 12 FL OZ CHICKEN STOCK (SEE PAGE 37)

SALT AND FRESHLY GROUND BLACK PEPPER

1 Heat the oil gently in a saucepan and sauté the onion in it, stirring until the onion becomes translucent. Break up the vermicelli with your fingers and add it to the onion. Continue to stir until the vermicelli becomes pale golden and aromatic, about 2-3 minutes.

2 Rinse the bulgar in a fine sieve under running water and add it to the pan. Stir to mix it in and add the chicken stock and seasoning. Cover the pan and simmer gently for about 7-8 minutes, until the mixture looks almost dry.

3 Cover with a kitchen towel, replace the lid on top and let it stand off the heat for at least 10-15 minutes. It can wait like this for about 1 hour. When you uncover it you will be surprised by its lovely aroma. Any leftovers can be successfully reheated the next day, with a little added water.

SERVES *4*

PREPARATION
10 minutes

COOKING
about 30 minutes

Calories per serving *350*
Total fat *Low*
Saturated fat *Low*
Protein *Low*
Carbohydrate *High*
Cholesterol *Nil*
Vitamins *B₁, B₃*
Minerals *Potassium, Iron*

COUSCOUS SALAD WITH PEACHES, ROCKET AND PINE NUTS

This salad full of sunny flavours is an improvisation of mine. Other fruit, such as melon, pears or strawberries, can be used instead of peaches. Served with soft cheeses – such as fresh goats' cheese, ricotta or Feta – and some fresh bread, it makes a lovely summer lunch particularly suited to a hot day. It also goes beautifully with marinated and grilled Haloumi cheese (see page 53).

85 G / **3** OZ PRE-COOKED COUSCOUS (MOST COUSCOUS NOWADAYS IS PRE-COOKED)

225 G / **8** OZ (**2** OR **3**) FIRM PEACHES, PEELED, STONED AND CUT INTO SMALL DICE

HANDFUL OF ROCKET LEAVES, TRIMMED AND CHOPPED COARSELY IF THEY ARE LARGE

possibly use watercress?

50 G / **2** OZ PINE NUTS

50 G / **2** OZ SKINNED ALMOND FLAKES

SMALL HANDFUL OF FRESH MINT, CHOPPED (RESERVING SOME SPRIGS FOR GARNISH)

FOR THE VINAIGRETTE:

3 TABLESPOONS HAZELNUT OR ALMOND OIL

1 TEASPOON SUNFLOWER OIL *(Canola)*

3 TABLESPOONS BALSAMIC VINEGAR

SALT

SERVES *4*

PREPARATION *30 minutes plus 1 hour's draining and 30 minutes' chilling*

Calories per serving *332*
Total fat *High*
Saturated fat *Low*
Protein *Low*
Carbohydrate *Low*
Cholesterol *Nil*
Vitamins *B₁, B₂, B₃, C, E*
Minerals *Iron, Zinc*

1 Soak the couscous in warm water for 15 minutes. Drain for about an hour to dry completely or roll it in a clean kitchen towel to absorb excess moisture.

2 Place the almond flakes in a dry frying pan over gentle heat and keep shaking the pan for 1-2 minutes, until the nuts are lightly browned all over. Do the same with the pine nuts. Set the toasted nuts aside.

3 Mix the vinaigrette ingredients well, preferably briefly in a blender. Taste and adjust by perhaps adding a little more vinegar.

(Couscous makes a rather submissive partner, so it needs livening up.)

4 Half an hour before serving, place everything but the toasted nuts in a large bowl and toss gently to coat the couscous in the vinaigrette. In the summer the salad is more refreshing served lightly chilled, so cover with film and place in the refrigerator at this stage.

5 To serve, mix in the toasted nuts, empty on a decorative platter (ideally a dark one to show the colours off) and decorate with the sprigs of mint.

Couscous Salad with Peaches, Rocket and Pine Nuts

Fish & Shellfish

PROVENÇAL SEAFOOD STEW

There is nothing more glorious than an exotic amalgam of different seafood on a plate, surrounded by a smooth aromatic sauce. Freshness is the most important factor, otherwise the result of even the most expensive ingredients is poor or simply uninteresting.

SERVES *4-6*

PREPARATION *20 minutes*

COOKING *about 1 hour*

Calories per serving *492*
Total fat *Low*
Saturated fat *Low*
Protein *High*
Carbohydrate *Low*
Cholesterol *249 mg*
Vitamins *A, B group, E*
Minerals *Calcium, Potassium, Iron, Zinc, Selenium, Iodine*

1-2 MEDIUM SQUID, PREPARED AS ON PAGE 75 BUT CUT INTO THIN RINGS
2 FILLETS OF JOHN DORY, RED BREAM, SEA BASS, HAKE OR COD, ABOUT 450 G / 1 LB IN TOTAL
2 FILLETS OF MONKFISH, ABOUT 450 G / 1 LB IN TOTAL
12 CLAMS, RINSED SEVERAL TIMES UNTIL CLEAN (OPTIONAL)
6-9 LANGOUSTINES OR RAW MEDITERRANEAN PRAWNS IN THEIR SHELLS
2 TABLESPOONS OLIVE OIL
3-4 SHALLOTS, PEELED AND CHOPPED
1 SMALL LEEK, CHOPPED
1 TABLESPOON FENNEL SEEDS
2 GARLIC CLOVES, CHOPPED
350 G / 12 OZ RIPE TOMATOES, PEELED AND CHOPPED

2 LARGE PINCHES OF SAFFRON THREADS, CRUMBLED
1 GLASS OF WHITE WINE
GRATED ZEST AND JUICE OF 1 UNCOATED ORANGE
2 TABLESPOONS FRESH DILL, PLUS MORE TO GARNISH
1.25 LITRES / 2 PINTS GOOD FISH STOCK
2-3 SPRIGS OF FRESH OREGANO, CHOPPED
1 COURGETTE
1 CARROT
SALT AND FRESHLY GROUND BLACK PEPPER

TO SERVE:
8 THIN SLICES OF FRENCH BAGUETTE, GRILLED UNTIL CRISP AND RUBBED WITH
2 GARLIC CLOVES
ROUILLE (PAGE 34)

1 Heat the oil gently in a large saucepan, add the shallots, leek and fennel seeds and sauté until the onion becomes translucent, about 5-7 minutes. Add the garlic and, a minute later, the tomatoes and saffron. Turn with a spatula until the tomatoes look wilted.

2 Add the wine, orange zest and juice, the dill and the stock. Season, cover and boil steadily for 20-30 minutes.

3 Liquidize the mixture in a food processor. Then press it through a fine sieve to extract all the juices. Pour the sieved mixture back into the pan, taste and adjust the seasoning.

4 Bring this back to the boil, add the squid rings and tentacles and cook gently for 15 minutes. Meanwhile, cut the fish into large cubes and add to the pan with the clams (if you are using them), langoustines or prawns and oregano. Cook for 5 minutes more.

5 In the meantime, slice the courgette and the carrot into long, thin, spaghetti-like strips and blanch them for 1 minute in lightly salted boiling water. Drain, and refresh in cold water.

6 Place a selection of seafood in each warmed soup plate and pour the sauce over it. Top with some snipped dill. Serve with strips of courgette and carrot, and baguette *croûtes* spread with rouille.

Provençal Seafood Stew

PSAROSOUPA
Aegean Fish Soup

A few years ago when I was travelling around the Greek islands with illustrator Linda Smith, collecting material for our book Greek Island Cookery, *we inevitably sampled a fish soup on every island. They were all wonderful, but also different. The one in Crete was made with* hristopsaro – *John Dory. In Rhodes, at the renowned Alexi's restaurant, theirs was made with grey mullet and tomatoes. On Alonnisos it is almost always made with the ferocious-looking bright-pink* skorpines – *scorpion fish – and never with tomatoes. In Mykonos it was made with the big-headed brown* rofos – *grouper – and so on. Basically they are all improvisations based on availability.*

When you are strolling round the waterfront in any of the Greek islands you will be dazzled by the fish on display at the restaurants. For a fish soup, all you have to do is choose your fish, have it weighed and then come back in half an hour and your meal is ready – because a Greek island fish soup makes a complete meal. The fish is cooked with vegetables – most often potatoes, carrots, courgettes and celery. The soup is then served separately and the fish surrounded by the vegetables brought on a platter.

In my opinion, the best soup is made with scorpion fish – in French rascasse rouge *and the main ingredient of the Provençal* bouillabaisse – *as its bones have a glutinous quality indispensable to a soup. Its huge head also adds a lot to the broth. A good alternative to this is red gurnard, which has a sweet taste. Dogfish is good and, of course, grey mullet; or a combination of different fish.*

Allow such fish to cook a little longer in order to get the full benefit of the tastes in the broth. This is particularly true with scorpion fish, which needs at least half an hour's steady boiling, or even more for larger specimens. If in doubt, make a broth first by boiling extra heads and bones of non-oily fish.

SERVES 6

PREPARATION *30 minutes*

COOKING
45-50 minutes

Calories per serving *386*

Total fat *Low*

Saturated fat *Low*

Protein *High*

Carbohydrate *Low*

Cholesterol *134 mg*

Vitamins *A, B group*

Minerals *Calcium, Potassium, Iron, Zinc, Selenium, Iodine*

1.75 KG / 4 LB MIXED FISH (SEE ABOVE), PREPARED WHOLE, RINSED AND DRAINED

2 TABLESPOONS OLIVE OIL, PLUS MORE TO SERVE

6-8 SMALL POTATOES, PEELED WHOLE

4-6 SMALL ONIONS, PEELED WHOLE

2 CARROTS, PEELED AND QUARTERED

1-2 SMALL STALKS OF CELERY, INCLUDING SOME LEAVES, CHOPPED

225 G / 8 OZ COURGETTES, QUARTERED INTO 5 CM / 2 IN LENGTHS

2 LEMONS

SALT AND FRESHLY GROUND BLACK PEPPER

1 Place the olive oil in a very large saucepan with 1.4 litres / 2½ pints of water, bring to the boil and boil rapidly for 4-5 minutes in order to emulsify the liquid.

2 Sprinkle in some seasoning and add the fish. Bring back to the boil and skim until clear.

Cover and cook for about 10 minutes.

3 Then add all the vegetables. They should be half-immersed in the broth, so add a little hot water if necessary but beware of too much liquid as it will result in a tasteless soup. Cook for 20-30 minutes for large fish or less for

smaller ones, making sure the fish does not disintegrate. It must hold together so that it can be taken out whole without breaking, if possible. If the fish are small and cook quicker, they should be taken out earlier and kept warm. Add in the juice of 1 lemon at the end.

4 Carefully take the fish out of the liquid, transfer it to a warmed platter and surround it with the vegetables. Serve the soup separately and ask people to help themselves to a piece of fish and a selection of vegetables; or, if they prefer, they can have the soup first and fish and vegetables afterwards. Offer some olive oil and lemon wedges for the fish.

TURBOT WITH GINGER AND SAFFRON

A sumptuous dish, this is at the same time one that is extremely simple to prepare. Other types of fish – such as steaks of halibut, hake, brill or monkfish – can be treated in the same manner and they are all quite captivating. Serve the fish with piles of bright-green mange-tout peas and broccoli florets, or the Fennel Gratin with Oil and Cheese on page 114.

4 TURBOT STEAKS, ABOUT **800** G / 1¾ LB IN TOTAL

2.5 CM / 1 IN PIECE OF FRESH ROOT GINGER, PEELED AND GRATED

2 LARGE PINCHES OF SAFFRON

2 TABLESPOONS OLIVE OIL

15 G / ½ OZ BUTTER

150 ML / ¼ PINT FISH STOCK, OR 1 GLASS OF DRY WHITE WINE

3 TABLESPOONS SINGLE CREAM

2 TABLESPOONS FINELY CHOPPED FRESH CORIANDER, PLUS SOME WHOLE SPRIGS FOR GARNISH

SALT AND FRESHLY GROUND BLACK PEPPER

SERVES *4*

PREPARATION *10-15 minutes*

COOKING *10-15 minutes*

Calories per serving *323*
Total fat *High*
Saturated fat *High*
Protein *High*
Carbohydrate *Low*
Cholesterol *15 mg*
Vitamins *B$_2$, B$_{12}$, B$_3$, B$_1$*
Minerals *Calcium, Potassium, Iron*

1 Wipe the fish clean. Heat the oil and butter gently in a large frying pan, add the ginger and sauté for a few seconds, turning with a wooden spatula.

2 Add the turbot steaks to the pan and turn them over a couple of times to coat them in the oil and ginger. Continue to sauté the fish in this manner for 3-4 minutes.

3 Add the stock or wine and some seasoning. Bring to a gentle boil and add the saffron, crushing it with your fingers. Simmer for 5-6 minutes (or barely 4 minutes for hake), basting the fish a few times.

4 Take the fish out and transfer to a warm serving platter. If there is excess liquid in the pan, boil it rapidly to reduce it. Add the cream and the chopped coriander and simmer gently and briefly (about 2 minutes), stirring and scraping the residue in the pan until the sauce has thickened lightly.

5 Pour the sauce over the fish, decorate with the reserved coriander sprigs and serve.

BAKED RED MULLET WITH ORANGE

Red mullet is undoubtedly the king of the Mediterranean. Although the Mediterranean types are smaller and more bony than others, they are also more tasty. Other fish can be cooked in this way, such as red snapper, sea bream, or even fillets of halibut, cod or haddock.

SERVES *4*

PREPARATION *10 minutes, plus 2 hours' marinating*

COOKING *30 minutes*

Calories per serving *380*
Total fat *Medium*
Saturated fat *Low*
Protein *High*
Carbohydrate *Low*
Cholesterol *Nil*
Vitamins *B group, C, E*
Minerals *Calcium, Potassium, Iron, Zinc, Selenium, Iodine*

4 WHOLE RED MULLETS OR 8 IF THEY ARE SMALL (ABOUT 1-1.5 KG / 2-3 LB TOTAL WEIGHT), CLEANED
3 LARGE JUICY ORANGES
FEW SPRIGS OF FRESH DILL

½ LEMON OR LIME
2 TABLESPOONS OLIVE OIL
2 TABLESPOONS TOASTED PINE NUTS
SALT

1 Ideally 2 hours ahead of cooking, place some fresh dill in the cavity of each fish and lay them side by side diagonally in a shallow oval oven dish, preferably glazed.
2 Squeeze the juice of 2 oranges as well as that of the lemon or lime. Mix these juices with the oil and pour over the fish. Leave to marinate for about 2 hours, spooning the marinade over the fish occasionally.

3 Preheat the oven to 180°C/350°F/gas 4. Just before cooking, sprinkle a little salt all over the fish. Cut half of the remaining orange into thin slices, quarter these and place a few quarters over each fish. Bake for 20 minutes.
4 Take out of the oven, baste, sprinkle pine nuts over and return to the oven for 10 minutes.
5 Serve garnished with dill and the remaining orange half cut into quarter slices.

BAKED PRAWNS WITH TOMATOES

SERVES *4*

PREPARATION *20 minutes*

COOKING *about 45 minutes*

Calories per serving *250*
Total fat *Medium*
Saturated fat *Medium*
Protein *High*
Carbohydrate *Low*
Cholesterol *209 mg*
Vitamins *A, B group, C, E*
Minerals *Calcium, Iron, Zinc, Selenium, Iodine*

400 G / 14 OZ PEELED TIGER OR KING PRAWNS
700 G / 1 LB 9 OZ RIPE TOMATOES, BLANCHED, SKINNED AND CHOPPED
115 G / 4 OZ FETA OR MOZZARELLA CHEESE, CUBED
2 TABLESPOONS OLIVE OIL

1 MEDIUM ONION, THINLY SLICED
1 GLASS OF DRY WHITE WINE
1 TEASPOON DRIED OREGANO
2 TABLESPOONS FINELY CHOPPED FRESH PARSLEY
SALT AND FRESHLY GROUND BLACK PEPPER

1 Preheat the oven to 180°C/350°F/gas 4. Heat the oil in a frying pan and sauté the onion gently until translucent. Add the wine and boil for 3-4 minutes.
2 Add the tomatoes, oregano and seasoning. Stir to mix everything and cook gently for 15-

20 minutes, stirring occasionally, until the sauce looks quite thick.
3 Mix in the prawns and parsley, empty the contents of the pan into an ovenproof dish and sprinkle the cheese cubes all over the top. Bake for 20 minutes. Serve hot.

Baked Red Mullet with Orange

SCALLOPS WITH MUSHROOMS

Scallops do not need a lot of cooking. Here, just searing quickly in a sparingly oiled frying pan is enough. An interesting variety of mushrooms alters the dish completely. The best is a mélange *of wild fungi.*

SERVES *4*

PREPARATION *20 minutes*

COOKING *about 10 minutes*

Calories per serving *185*
Total fat *High*
Saturated fat *Low*
Protein *High*
Carbohydrate *Low*
Cholesterol *35 mg*
Vitamins *A, B group, C, E*
Minerals *Potassium, Iron, Zinc, Selenium, Iodine*

10 SCALLOPS, SHELLED, RINSED AND DRAINED
2 GARLIC CLOVES, PEELED AND CRUSHED
225 G / 8 OZ FIRM CHESTNUT OR OTHER MUSHROOMS
3 TABLESPOONS OLIVE OIL
1 RED SWEET PEPPER, DESEEDED AND CUBED
2 TABLESPOONS FINELY CHOPPED PARSLEY
1 TABLESPOON FINELY CHOPPED CHERVIL
SALT AND FRESHLY GROUND BLACK PEPPER

1 Separate any corals from the scallops and set them aside. Slice each scallop horizontally into two flat discs. Brush some olive oil over a ridged heavy cast-iron frying pan or a non-stick frying pan and over the scallops.
2 Place the remaining olive oil in another frying pan and, when it is hot, add the sliced mushrooms and the peppers and stir over medium heat for 5-6 minutes.
3 Add some seasoning, the corals, the garlic and the herbs and cook for 2-3 minutes longer.
4 While the mushrooms and peppers are cooking, heat the pan for the scallops and, when it is almost smoking, put in the scallops and allow them a minute on each side at most.
5 Toss into the mushroom mix and serve.

SQUID IN WINE SAUCE

SERVES *4 as a main course, or 6 as a first course*

PREPARATION *20 minutes*

COOKING *about 1 hour*

Calories per serving *452*
Total fat *Medium*
Saturated fat *Low*
Protein *High*
Carbohydrate *Low*
Cholesterol *844 mg*
Vitamins *B group, E*
Minerals *Potassium, Iron, Zinc, Selenium, Iodine*

1.5 KG / 3½ LB MEDIUM-SIZED SQUID (ABOUT 3 OR 4)
2 GLASSES OF DRY WHITE WINE
350 G / 12 OZ SLICED ONIONS
3 TABLESPOONS OLIVE OIL
150 ML / ¼ PINT HOT WATER
2 STAR ANISE (OPTIONAL)
SALT AND FRESHLY GROUND BLACK PEPPER
3 TABLESPOONS CHOPPED PARSLEY OR CHERVIL

1 First clean the squid: pull the head away from the body and pull the fins away from the body. Open the bodies up and discard all the innards. Pull off the outer skin and discard. Slice each head across and keep the tentacles, discarding the rest of the head. Rinse everything carefully, removing all traces of sand. Slice each body in half lengthwise and then cut into strips about 2.5 cm / 1 in wide.
2 Sauté the onions in the olive oil in a saucepan over moderate heat. When the onions start to colour, add the squid and star anise if you are using it. Sauté them, stirring constantly, until all the water produced has evaporated and the squid starts to colour. This will take about 15 minutes in all.
3 Slowly add the wine and, when the steam subsides, add the water and seasoning. Cover and cook slowly for about 20-30 minutes, until tender (depending on the size of the squid). It may start to stick, so stir occasionally and add a little more water as needed. You should be left with a delicious sweet thick sauce.
4 Add the herbs, cook for 2 minutes and serve.

MEJILLONES A LA MARINERA
Mussels with Garlic and Wine

Mussels prepared quickly, as here, are served all over the Mediterranean, although they are most associated with France and Spain. Any good tapas *bar will display mussels among its intriguing array of appetizers. This recipe is almost identical to French* moules marinières, *but for the addition of saffron. In countries such as Greece and Turkey there is a whole range of dishes with mussels. Once they have been prepared and cooked quickly, almost in the same way as here, they are then shelled and made into delicious pilaffs or dipped into garlicky breadcrumbs and fried or grilled. In Turkey, large mussels are stuffed with a delicious rice stuffing involving tiny currants and pine nuts.*

1.3 KG / 3½ LB MUSSELS
2 GARLIC CLOVES, PEELED AND CRUSHED
150 ML / ¼ PINT WHITE WINE
2 TABLESPOONS OLIVE OIL
3-4 SHALLOTS OR 1 MEDIUM ONION, THINLY SLICED
2-3 SPRIGS OF FRESH THYME, CHOPPED

2-3 SMALL TOMATOES, SKINNED AND DICED (OPTIONAL)
LARGE PINCH OF SAFFRON THREADS, CRUMBLED
FRESHLY GROUND PEPPER
2 TABLESPOONS FINELY CHOPPED CHERVIL OR PARSLEY, TO GARNISH

SERVES *4*

PREPARATION *about 30 minutes*

COOKING *10-15 minutes, plus 5 minutes' standing*

Calories per serving *333*
Total fat *Medium*
Saturated fat *Low*
Protein *High*
Carbohydrate *Low*
Cholesterol *133 mg*
Vitamins *B group, E*
Minerals *Calcium, Potassium, Iron, Zinc, Selenium, Iodine*

1 Wash the mussels under running water, scraping them with a knife to remove barnacles and beards. Place them in a sink or bowl filled with water for 10 minutes, letting their grit sink and lift them out by hand. Repeat this process several times until the water is clear. At the same time, get rid of any mussels with broken shells or any which remain open when they are tapped.

2 Heat the oil in a large saucepan, add the shallots or onion and sauté until glistening. Add the garlic and thyme. Sauté together until the mixture is aromatic, then add the tomatoes if you are using them (they do add sweetness) and stir for 2 minutes.

3 Pour in the wine. Add some pepper and the saffron. Let the mixture bubble for 2-3 minutes, then add the mussels. Turn the heat up, cover and cook briskly for 4-5 minutes, shaking the pan vigorously a few times, until the mussels have opened. Take the mussels out with a slotted spoon and place them in a large warmed bowl. Discard any mussels which remain closed.

4 Let the cooking liquid stand for 5 minutes to let any grit sink to the bottom. Ideally the liquid should be strained through cheesecloth over the mussels at this stage. Otherwise tilt the pan carefully and pour the liquid out, leaving behind any gritty traces. Sprinkle the herbs over the top and serve immediately in soup bowls, offering plenty of crusty bread.

HAKE IN RED PEPPER COULIS

Mediterranean hake has a subtle, clean taste which is often used as a background to playful flavours and textures. It is commonly served baked with pepper and tomato sauce, in Spain it becomes merluza en salsa verde *and in this recipe it is combined with a Provençal explosion of colour and tastes in a red pepper coulis. Fillets of John Dory or sea bass can also be served in the same way. This dish goes well with the Catalan Spinach on page 117.*

SERVES *4*

PREPARATION *about 30 minutes*

COOKING *about 10 minutes*

Calories per serving *282*
Total fat *Medium*
Saturated fat *Low*
Protein *High*
Carbohydrate *Low*
Cholesterol *40 mg*
Vitamins *A, Folate, B6, C, E*
Minerals *Iron, Potassium*

4 HAKE FILLETS, EACH WEIGHING ABOUT 175 G / 6 OZ, OR 8 SMALLER FILLETS ABOUT 85-115 G / 3-4 OZ
2 TABLESPOONS OLIVE OIL
2 GARLIC CLOVES, PEELED AND CRUSHED
1 SMALL GLASS OF WHITE WINE
HANDFUL OF BASIL LEAVES

SALT AND FRESHLY GROUND BLACK PEPPER
LEMON SLICES, TO GARNISH

FOR THE RED PEPPER COULIS:
3 MEDIUM-SIZED RED SWEET PEPPERS
1 TEASPOON OLIVE OIL
1½ TABLESPOONS BALSAMIC VINEGAR

1 First make the coulis: preheat a moderate grill. Place the peppers in the grill pan, arrange them about 5 cm / 2 in from the heat and grill them for about 10 minutes, turning 2-3 times until charred evenly all over.

2 When the peppers are cool enough to handle, peel or scrape off their charred skins as neatly as possible and discard. Trim and discard their tops as well as their seeds and any thick inner membranes.

3 Place all the pepper flesh and their juices in a food processor with a little hot water, and process to a smooth paste. Put this through a fine sieve, pressing and scraping to get all the juices through. Add the oil and vinegar, and mix them in. Cover the coulis and set aside.

4 Now cook the fish: heat the oil gently in a large sauté pan, add the garlic and stir briefly. Then add the fillets, skin-side down, and sauté gently for 2 minutes without allowing them to brown. Immediately add the wine, most of the basil, torn by hand, and salt and pepper. Tilt the pan to coat the fish and cook gently for 3-4 more minutes, basting the fish a couple of times. Hake really needs very little cooking.

5 Lift the fillets from the pan and transfer to individual warmed plates. Reduce the juices in the pan by boiling rapidly for a couple of minutes and pour them over the fillets. Surround each fillet with the coulis and garnish with the remaining basil leaves and some lemon slices.

Hake in Red Pepper Coulis

NORTH AFRICAN MONKFISH

Monkfish, with its layer of tastes and its wonderful texture, always produces astounding dishes. However, this must be the best and the easiest of them all, and has been a favourite of anyone who has tried it.

SERVES *4*

PREPARATION *20 minutes*

COOKING *about 15 minutes*

Calories per serving *148*
Total fat *High*
Saturated fat *Low*
Protein *High*
Carbohydrate *Low*
Cholesterol *14 mg*
Vitamins *B₃*
Minerals *Iron, Iodine*

2 MONKFISH TAILS, SKINNED, MEMBRANE REMOVED, BONED AND FILLETED INTO 4 LONG FILLETS (ABOUT 1.25 KG / 3 LB ON THE BONE)
3 TABLESPOONS OLIVE OIL
2-3 GARLIC CLOVES, PEELED AND CRUSHED

2.5 CM / 1 IN PIECE OF FRESH ROOT GINGER, PEELED AND GRATED
1 TABLESPOON GROUND CUMIN
LARGE HANDFUL OF CORIANDER, FINELY CHOPPED
SALT AND FRESHLY GROUND BLACK PEPPER

1 Rinse and dry the fish. It is important to dry it properly; otherwise it will produce a lot of moisture while cooking – and it should not be swimming in a bath of water. Cut each fillet into 3-4 large cubes – about double bite-sized.
2 Heat the oil gently in a large frying pan. Add the garlic, sauté briefly until aromatic and immediately add the ginger. After a few seconds, add the cumin while stirring continuously. The mixture should not burn, but the cumin oils will become aromatic.
3 Turn the heat up in order to seal the fish.

Add the fish and keep stirring to coat it all in this mixture. Let it cook for about 6-8 minutes (monkfish is quite a muscular fish), stirring gently from time to time. Once the fish is sealed turn the heat down. When the fish is cooked to your liking (take a piece out and try it, as it should not be hard at this stage), add salt, pepper and the coriander and stir quickly for 2 or 3 minutes more. It should be quite dry by then, but with a delicious sauce.
4 Serve with spinach or leeks and small boiled potatoes, or with a large colourful salad.

SWORDFISH BROCHETTES

There is excitement whenever a kaiki with a huge swordfish on board comes into the small harbour of Patitiri on the Aegean island of Alonnisos. Sometimes two or three children will be seen carrying the glistening creature to a particular restaurant. Apart from feasting our eyes, it also means feasting our palates in the evening, as xifias souvlaki, or swordfish brochettes, will be featured in most restaurants. If the souvlakia are to be served al fresco, a large salad and lots of fresh bread will be accompaniments enough; otherwise serve the skewers with steamed broccoli and boiled potatoes.

SERVES *4*

PREPARATION *15 minutes, plus 4-5 hours' marinating*

COOKING *4-8 minutes*

900 G / 2 LB SWORDFISH
2 TABLESPOONS OLIVE OIL
JUICE OF 1½ LEMONS
SMALL BUNCH OF FRESH MARJORAM, FINELY

CHOPPED, OR 1 TABLESPOON DRIED OREGANO
2 GREEN SWEET PEPPERS
1 RED ONION, PEELED AND QUARTERED
SALT AND FRESHLY GROUND BLACK PEPPER

1 Slice the fish into large bite-sized cubes. Beat the oil, lemon juice, herbs and seasoning together and toss the fish in this until it is well coated. Cover and leave to marinate for 3-4 hours in the refrigerator.

2 Slice the peppers into quarters, trim them and discard the seeds and stalks. If the quarters are too large, slice each one across the middle. Take the onion layers apart.

3 About 30 minutes before the fish is to be cooked, thread the cubes on 4-6 metal skewers, alternating with one piece of onion and one of pepper. Brush all the food on the skewers with the marinade.

4 Grill the souvlakia briefly on charcoal for about 3-4 minutes on each side, or grill under an ordinary grill (placing them not too near the heat) for 2-3 minutes only on each side. Once they have been turned over, brush them again with the marinade to keep them moist.

Calories per serving 309
Total fat *Low*
Saturated fat *Low*
Protein *High*
Carbohydrate *Low*
Cholesterol 99 *mg*
Vitamins *B group, E*
Minerals *Potassium, Iron, Iodine*

SPICY GRILLED TUNA WITH ROCKET

There is something spectacular about a fresh tuna steak scorching over a charcoal fire by the sea in September. Tuna – with its rich flavours – responds well to marinades and needs to be accompanied by something that provides a sharp contrast. If rocket is unavailable, use watercress instead.

4 THIN TUNA STEAKS, EACH ABOUT 150 G / 5 OZ
BUNCH OF ROCKET OR 115 G / 4 OZ ROCKET LEAVES
1 TABLESPOON OLIVE OIL

FOR THE MARINADE:
1 TABLESPOON OLIVE OIL

JUICE OF 1-2 LARGE LEMONS
2 GARLIC CLOVES, PEELED AND CRUSHED
2 CM / ¾ IN PIECE OF FRESH ROOT GINGER, GRATED
½ TEASPOON GROUND CUMIN
HANDFUL OF FRESH CORIANDER, FINELY CHOPPED
SALT AND FRESHLY GROUND BLACK PEPPER

SERVES 4

PREPARATION 15 *minutes, plus 3-4 hours' marinating*

COOKING *4-8 minutes*

Calories per serving 263
Total fat *High*
Saturated fat *Low*
Protein *High*
Carbohydrate *Low*
Cholesterol 39 *mg*
Vitamins *B group*
Minerals *Potassium, Iron, Zinc, Selenium, Iodine*

1 Lay the tuna in one layer on a platter. Beat the marinade ingredients together with some seasoning and pour this over the steaks. Cover and chill in the refrigerator for 3-4 hours, turning the steaks over a couple of times.

2 Grilling over charcoal in the open air always has the best results. Lift the steaks from the marinade and place them in one of those special barbecue racks which close over them and hold them in place. This will prevent them from breaking up. Grill for about 3-4 minutes on each side, according to how hot your barbecue is. Alternatively, if you are using a conventional grill, cook them very quickly under a high heat, about 1-2 minutes on each side, so that they are still juicy in the middle. Tuna goes papery when overcooked.

3 While the tuna is cooking, boil the marinade in a small pan to reduce it a little.

4 At the last minute, heat the oil gently in a frying pan and toss the rocket in it rapidly. It should only turn bright green and wilt and not cook – this takes less than 1 minute.

5 Divide the rocket between 4 plates and place the steaks on top of it. Dribble the marinade over the steaks and serve.

Meat & Poultry

OSSOBUCO ALLA ROMANA
Roman Braised Shin of Veal

Ossobuchi *are medium-thick slices of a shin of veal which are braised slowly until they are meltingly sweet.* Ossobuco *always constitutes a treat, with its tantalizing taste and pampering texture. Originally a Milanese dish – the name actually means 'bone with a hole', according to Marcella Hazan – it contains tomatoes and it is traditionally served with* risotto alla Milanese, *a saffron and bone marrow risotto.*

A long time ago we had a very different version in a small lunch-time restaurant almost under the shade of the Vatican in Rome. To my mind this was the purest version I ever had and this is now the only way I cook it. Served with delicious spinach and sautéed potatoes, it was much simpler and lighter. Here it is – a purist's dish.

SERVES *4*

PREPARATION
10 minutes

COOKING
about 1¾ hours

Calories per serving *367*
Total fat *Low*
Saturated fat *Low*
Protein *High*
Carbohydrate *Low*
Cholesterol *130 mg*
Vitamins *B group, E*
Minerals *Potassium, Iron, Zinc, Selenium, Iodine*

4 PIECES OF OSSOBUCO, EACH ABOUT 2.5 CM / 1 IN THICK (TOTAL WEIGHT ABOUT 1 KG / 2¼ LB)

2 TABLESPOONS OLIVE OIL

2 TABLESPOONS PLAIN FLOUR

5-6 FRESH SAGE LEAVES

150 ML / ¼ PINT DRY WHITE WINE

450 ML / ¾ PINT HOT BEEF OR CHICKEN STOCK

FEW LONG PIECES OF FRESH OR DRIED ORANGE PEEL (FROM AN UNCOATED ORANGE)

5-6 BASIL LEAVES, TORN BY HAND

SALT AND FRESHLY GROUND BLACK PEPPER

1 Choose a large and heavy-based casserole or other pan with a tight-fitting lid which will take the ossobuco in a single layer and heat the oil in it. Pat the meat dry and coat it lightly in flour. Shake off excess flour and, when the oil is quite hot, brown the meat quickly on both sides. It should be light golden.

2 Once the meat is ready, add the sage leaves and a minute later pour in the wine. Let it bubble and evaporate for a few minutes, then add the stock, the orange peel and seasoning to taste. Cover tightly and cook very gently for about 1½ hours, until the meat is very soft. Turn the meat over carefully a couple of times during the cooking time, but be careful not to spill the marrow from its centre.

3 Once the meat is ready, sprinkle the basil leaves over it, cover again and simmer for a few more minutes. By now the sauce will be thick and velvety. Serve with Catalan Spinach (page 117) or steamed small courgettes and mashed potatoes made with olive oil instead of butter.

Ossobuco alla Romana

BULGUR KEBABI
Minced Lamb and Cracked Wheat Kebabs

SERVES 6

PREPARATION 20
minutes, plus 30
minutes' soaking

COOKING
about 12 minutes

Calories per serving 453
Total fat High
Saturated fat Low
Protein High
Carbohydrate Low
Cholesterol 46 mg
Vitamins A, B group, E
Minerals Potassium, Iron,
Zinc

1 KG / 2¼ LB LEAN MINCED LAMB

85 G / 3 OZ FINE BULGAR (CRACKED WHEAT)

1 EGG

1 LARGE ONION, COARSELY GRATED

3 GARLIC CLOVES, CRUSHED

4 TABLESPOONS FINELY CHOPPED FRESH MINT

5 SPRIGS OF FLAT-LEAVED PARSLEY, FINELY CHOPPED

½ TEASPOON GROUND ALLSPICE

1½ TEASPOONS PAPRIKA

½ TEASPOON CAYENNE OR ANTEP PEPPER

40 G / 1½ OZ PINE NUTS, COARSELY CHOPPED

SALT AND FRESHLY GROUND BLACK PEPPER

TO SERVE:

HOT FLAT PITTA BREAD

THINLY SLICED ONION RINGS, SPRINKLED WITH URFA
PEPPER (SEE PAGE 15)

GRILLED TOMATO SLICES

SMALL PLATE OF ANTEP PEPPER (SEE PAGE 15)

1 Rinse the bulgar briefly. Put in a bowl, cover with hot water and leave to soak for 20 minutes. Drain and squeeze out excess water.
2 Mix the bulgar with the meat and the egg, and then mix in the remaining ingredients. Season the mixture and work it with your hands until it is well amalgamated. Make it into 18 medium-sized elongated flat patties.

3 Grill the patties in 2 batches, for about 3 minutes on each side. Keep the first batch warm while the second is cooking.
4 While the kebabs are grilling, prepare a small platter with some onion rings sprinkled with urfa pepper. Serve with hot pitta, grilled tomatoes, small plates of antep pepper for dipping the kebabs in, and a large mixed salad.

ALBONDIGAS
Spanish Meatballs

Albondigas *are ubiquitous in Spain, as they are to be found on every bar among the* tapas.

MAKES 30-35 small
meatballs

PREPARATION 20-25
minutes

COOKING
40 minutes

675 G / 1½ LB MINCED BEEF (OR LAMB AND BEEF)

1 MEDIUM ONION, COARSELY GRATED

3 GARLIC CLOVES, PEELED AND CRUSHED

1 EGG

2 TABLESPOONS GROUND ALMONDS

1 TABLESPOON PIMENTÓN DULCE (SEE PAGE 14) OR
PAPRIKA

1 TABLESPOON GROUND CUMIN

¼ TEASPOON GROUND CINNAMON

4 TABLESPOONS FINELY CHOPPED PARSLEY

FOR THE SAUCE:

2 TABLESPOONS GROUNDNUT OIL

2 TABLESPOONS FENNEL SEEDS

1 GLASS OF WHITE WINE

2 TABLESPOONS ANISE, PERNOD OR RICARD

400 G / 14 OZ TIN OF CHOPPED TOMATOES

1 TABLESPOON TOMATO PASTE

1 Mix all the ingredients for the meatballs in a large bowl. Take small handfuls of the mixture and shape them into walnut-sized balls.

2 Next make the sauce: heat the oil gently in a large heavy pan with a lid, add the fennel seeds and swirl them around until they start to sizzle. Add the wine and the anise and bubble for 2 minutes. Add the tomatoes with their liquid, the tomato paste diluted in 150 ml / ¼ pint of water, and seasoning. Simmer gently for 10 minutes.

3 Add the meatballs and roll to coat in the sauce. Cover and simmer for 20-30 minutes. Turn them over carefully once during that time and add a little water if needed.

Calories per meatball *52*
Total fat *High*
Saturated fat *High*
Protein *High*
Carbohydrate *Low*
Cholesterol *10 mg*
Vitamins B_3, B_6, B_{12}, *E*
Minerals *Iron, Zinc*

MOROCCAN GRILLED KOFTA

900 G / 2 LB MINCED LAMB (OR LAMB AND BEEF)
1 LARGE ONION, COARSELY GRATED
2.5 CM / 1 IN PIECE OF FRESH GINGER, PEELED AND GRATED
1 TABLESPOON GROUND CUMIN
1 TEASPOON GROUND CORIANDER
½ TEASPOON ALLSPICE

½ TEASPOON RAS-EL-HANOUT (OPTIONAL, PAGE 23)
¼ TEASPOON CAYENNE PEPPER
1 TEASPOON PAPRIKA
1 EGG
4 TABLESPOONS FINELY CHOPPED PARSLEY
4 TABLESPOONS FINELY CHOPPED FRESH CORIANDER
SALT AND FRESHLY GROUND BLACK PEPPER

SERVES *4*

PREPARATION *25 minutes, plus 1-2 hours' resting*

COOKING *10-12 minutes*

Calories per serving *378*
Total fat *High*
Saturated fat *Low*
Protein *High*
Carbohydrate *Low*
Cholesterol *58 mg*
Vitamins *A, B group*
Minerals *Potassium, Iron, Zinc*

1 The mince used ideally should have been through the mincing machine twice. Greek butchers do that automatically and this results in a much better blended kofta and a more pleasing all-in-one softer texture. Combine all the ingredients in a bowl, season and mix vigorously with your hands in order to blend properly and achieve a silky texture. Cover and rest for 1-2 hours in the refrigerator.

2 Shape the rested mixture into sausage shapes, about 10 cm / 4 in long and pass a flat metal skewer through the middle of each. Arrange 2-3 of these on each skewer. Squeeze the meat around the skewer in order to make it thinner and longer and squeeze the 2 edges in so that it stays firmly on the skewer. They should not be too heavy or they will fall off.

3 Grill the kebabs, either over charcoal or in the kitchen under a preheated grill on a lightly oiled grilling pan for 10-12 minutes in all, turning them carefully around 2-3 times until they are crisp and golden all over.

CHICKEN WITH FORTY CLOVES OF GARLIC

I still remember the first time we had a dish similar to this, cooked with rabbit by Jill Norman, the cookery editor and publisher, who is also an imaginative and skilful cook. When the casserole was brought to the dinner table and its lid lifted, the aromas that engulfed us were sensational.

In Provence, lamb is also baked with this amount of garlic underneath it. The dish is in a class by itself when the garlic used is young and fresh, with pink plump juicy cloves. When the garlic is old it becomes almost acrid and rather bitter-tasting, particularly when roasted.

The chicken can be roasted whole or cut into pieces beforehand for the sake of convenience.

1 OVEN-READY CHICKEN, WEIGHING ABOUT **1.25 KG /
3¼ LB**, WHOLE OR CUT INTO **4-6** PIECES
40 GARLIC CLOVES, UNPEELED
3 TABLESPOONS OLIVE OIL
2 CARROTS, SLICED
2 TABLESPOONS COARSELY CHOPPED TARRAGON

3-4 SPRIGS OF FRESH THYME, COARSELY CHOPPED
2 TABLESPOONS BRANDY
1 GLASS OF WHITE WINE, SUCH AS A WHITE CÔTES-DU-RHÔNE
SALT AND FRESHLY GROUND BLACK PEPPER

SERVES *4*

PREPARATION *10 minutes*

COOKING *about 1¾ hours*

Calories per serving *259*
Total fat *Low*
Saturated fat *Low*
Protein *High*
Carbohydrate *Low*
Cholesterol *171 mg*
Vitamins *B group*
Minerals *Potassium, Iron, Zinc, Sellenium, Iodine*

1 Preheat the oven to 160°C/325°F/gas 3. Heat the oil gently in a large heavy-based ovenproof casserole. Place the chicken or chicken pieces in it and sauté for 8-10 minutes, turning until light golden all over. Remove the chicken and transfer to a plate.
2 Place the garlic, carrots and herbs in the casserole and sauté them for 3-4 minutes, turning with a spatula.
3 Put the chicken back in the casserole and pour over the brandy and the wine. Allow to bubble for 3-4 minutes. Sprinkle in some

seasoning, cover tightly and cook in the oven for 1½ hours.
4 Take the casserole to the table and lift the lid there for the full aromatic effect. Serve the chicken with some of the garlic cloves, which will have become quite creamy inside and should be squeezed out of their shells either on the chicken or on bread. Lightly steamed crunchy French beans go perfectly with this dish, also some plain boiled small potatoes for those with large appetites.

Chicken with Forty Cloves of Garlic

MAGRET OF DUCK WITH POMEGRANATES

The arrival of autumn is signalled for me when the scarlet pomegranates look bulging on the trees in September. By October, in an area as beautiful as Pelion in Greece, the landscape looks transformed. The leaves are turning all the shades of copper and starting to fall on the mossy ground. The brilliantly coloured fruit then looks even more glorious on the trees. Pomegranates, quinces and apples hanging on the boughs amidst the autumnal riot of colours and mellow light attain a quite magical quality.

At this time of the year I love visiting my sister at her house in Tsangaratha in Pelion and there we indulge ourselves in seasonal follies. Everything we cook has some of the fruit from the garden and to crown it all in the evening we roast chestnuts on the fire. Utter seasonal bliss.

SERVES *4*

PREPARATION *25 minutes*

COOKING *45-50 minutes*

Calories per serving *359*
Total fat *High*
Saturated fat *Medium*
Protein *High*
Carbohydrate *Low*
Cholesterol *186 mg*
Vitamins *B group*
Minerals *Iron, Zinc, Potassium*

4 MAGRETS (DUCK BREASTS), TOTAL WEIGHT ABOUT
675 G / 1½ LB, OR 2 LARGE ONES
1½ TABLESPOONS AROMATIC HONEY
2 TABLESPOONS LEMON JUICE
PINCH OF GROUND CINNAMON
SALT AND FRESHLY GROUND BLACK PEPPER

FOR THE POMEGRANATE SAUCE:
SEEDS FROM 2 POMEGRANATES, WITHOUT THE
YELLOW PITH (SEE PAGE 19)
2 SHALLOTS, SLICED
2 TABLESPOONS OLIVE OIL
1 GLASS OF AMONTILLADO OR FINO SHERRY
1 TABLESPOON BALSAMIC VINEGAR

1 Prepare the sauce in advance (the duck breasts have to be cooked just before they are to be served). Sauté the shallots in the oil over gentle heat until translucent. Add the sherry, let it bubble for 2 minutes and then add the pomegranate seeds and any reserved juices. Simmer for 15 minutes and let it cool a little.

2 Liquidize the sauce in a blender or food processor and pass it through a fine sieve. Pour back into the pan and set aside.

3 Preheat the oven to 220°C/425°F/gas 7. Trim excess fat from the magrets and wipe them with kitchen paper. Using a small sharp knife, score the skins with a criss-cross pattern. Season and place them side by side on a rack, skin-side down over a roasting pan.

4 Half an hour before they are to be served, place the magrets in the oven and cook for 10 minutes. Take out and drain off all the fat.

5 Beat the remaining ingredients together with some seasoning and paint this over the breasts generously. Turn the magrets over skin-side up and brush this side also. Cook for 15-20 minutes more, according to size and individual taste (but they should still be pink in the middle).

6 Just before serving, finish the sauce: add the juices from the duck, season and simmer for 5 minutes. Finally add the vinegar.

7 Warm 4 plates. Cut each breast into slices and arrange them in the middle of each plate. Surround with the pomegranate sauce and serve with steamed fine French green beans and small boiled potatoes.

Magret of Duck with Pomegranates

MARINATED GRILLED POUSSIN

The trick with this delicious and easy dish is to organize yourself well in advance, as the marinating accounts for the tantalizing flavours. It is best if you can marinate overnight, or at least for 6 hours.

This makes an ideal summer dish, served with a large and colourful salad of different leaves, such as Cos, frisée, radicchio and some rocket and fennel with spring onions. If you would like to make the meal even more impressive, it goes well with strips of roasted peppers dressed with olive oil and balsamic vinegar.

SERVES *4*

PREPARATION *30 minutes, plus overnight marinating*

COOKING *10-15 minutes*

Calories per serving *315*
Total fat *High*
Saturated fat *Medium*
Protein *High*
Carbohydrate *Low*
Cholesterol *149 mg*
Vitamins *B group*
Minerals *Iron, Zinc, Potassium, Selenium*

4 POUSSINS, CUT INTO TWO LENGTHWISE

FOR THE MARINADE:
3 TABLESPOONS OLIVE OIL
2.5 CM / 1 IN PIECE OF FRESH ROOT GINGER, PEELED AND FINELY GRATED
2 GARLIC CLOVES, CRUSHED
JUICE OF 1 LARGE LEMON
1 TEASPOON FRESH OR DRIED OREGANO OR THYME
SALT AND FRESHLY GROUND BLACK PEPPER

1 Lay the chicken halves on a flat platter, skin-side up. Beat the marinade ingredients together lightly and, using a spoon, spread some over each piece of chicken. Leave to stand for about 30 minutes. Turn each piece over and repeat the process, making sure that most surfaces are coated. Cover with film and place in the fridge overnight if possible.
2 Preheat the grill, place the chicken pieces on a grilling rack, skin-side down, and grill under a low-to-medium heat for about 5-6 minutes or until they start to brown. Turn over, brush with some of the marinade juices and cook slowly for 6-8 minutes until the skin starts to blister. If you have to cook them in 2 batches, keep the first batch hot in a low oven while cooking the remaining pieces.
3 Alternatively, make the meal informal and encourage people to start eating the chicken as it comes straight from the grill.

LAMB AND COS LETTUCE CASSEROLE

One of the best dishes in Greek cooking, this is found on the islands and the mainland alike in the spring, around Easter. If one meat dish were to represent each Mediterranean country this should be the one for Greece. It is made with a leg of lamb, which is leaner than a shoulder; however, the latter can be used trimmed. Serve with fresh crusty bread.

SERVES *4-6*

PREPARATION *20 minutes*

COOKING *about 1½ hours*

1 KG / 2¼ LB BONED LEG OF LAMB, CUBED LARGE
2 LARGE COS LETTUCES, SHREDDED
2 TABLESPOONS SUNFLOWER OIL
1 MEDIUM ONION, THINLY SLICED
4-5 SPRING ONIONS, CHOPPED
900 ML / 1⅔ PINT HOT WATER
4 TABLESPOONS COARSELY CHOPPED FRESH DILL
EGG-AND-LEMON SAUCE (PAGE 36)
SALT

1 Wipe the meat clean. Heat the oil in a large heavy-based pan and sauté the onions until glistening. Turn the heat up, add the meat and sauté, stirring, for about 10 minutes or until all the liquid evaporates.

2 Add the hot water and some salt, cover and cook for 50-60 minutes, until the meat is tender but not falling apart. Mix in the lettuces, spring onions and the dill, cover and cook gently for 15 more minutes.

3 Let the dish stand for 5 minutes before adding the egg sauce. Beat the eggs lightly, add the cornflour and beat until smooth. Add the lemon juice and beat together briefly. Then gradually add 4-5 tablespoons of the hot liquid, while beating continuously.

4 Pour the sauce over the meat and rotate the pan, until well incorporated. Return to a gentle heat for 1-2 minutes, just to warm the sauce through without allowing it to boil.

Calories per serving *423*
Total fat *High*
Saturated fat *Low*
Protein *High*
Carbohydrate *Low*
Cholesterol *99 mg*
Vitamins *A, B group, C, E*
Minerals *Potassium, Iron, Zinc, Iodine*

MOROCCAN CHICKEN TAJINE

1 FREE-RANGE CHICKEN, WEIGHING ABOUT **1.25** KG / **3¼** LB, CUT INTO **6-8** PIECES

2 TABLESPOONS OLIVE OIL

1 LARGE ONION, THINLY SLICED

5 GARLIC CLOVES, PEELED AND CRUSHED

2.5 CM / **1** IN PIECE OF FRESH GINGER, GRATED

2 PINCHES OF SAFFRON THREADS, CRUMBLED

1 TABLESPOON CARAWAY SEEDS

1½ TABLESPOONS GROUND CUMIN

1 TEASPOON PAPRIKA

¼ TEASPOON CAYENNE PEPPER

150 ML / **¼** PINT HOT WATER

1 PRESERVED LEMON (PAGE **19**), FINELY CHOPPED

LARGE HANDFUL OF CORIANDER, COARSELY CHOPPED

225 G / **8** OZ BLACK OLIVES, RINSED

SALT AND FRESHLY GROUND BLACK PEPPER

FOR THE COUSCOUS:

275 G / **10** OZ PRE-COOKED COUSCOUS

1 TABLESPOON OLIVE OIL

300 ML / **½** PINT HOT CHICKEN BROTH OR WATER

1 Heat the oil in a large ovenproof saucepan and sauté the onion until translucent. Add the garlic, ginger and spices and sauté together briefly until aromatic. Add the chicken pieces and turn them around with a spatula for 2-3 minutes to coat them in the spices. Add the hot water and the preserved lemon with some seasoning. Cover and either simmer for 50 minutes or cook in the oven preheated to 160°C/325°F/gas 3 for 1 hour.

2 Add the coriander and the olives to the pan and simmer for 10 more minutes or return to the oven for 15 minutes more.

3 Half an hour before serving, prepare the couscous: spread it in a large attractive gratin dish, add the oil with some salt and the broth or water. Mix and let it stand for 15 minutes. Fluff it a little with a fork and place in the oven with the chicken for 5 minutes just to warm it through.

SERVES *4*

PREPARATION
20 minutes

COOKING
1¼-1¾ hours

Calories per serving *519*
Total fat *Medium*
Saturated fat *Low*
Protein *High*
Carbohydrate *Low*
Cholesterol *105 mg*
Vitamins *B group, E*
Minerals *Iron, Potassium, Selenium*

Vegetables
& Pulses

IMAM BAYILDI
Turkish-style Baked Aubergines

Everyone will have heard about the Turkish Imam fainting after indulging in this dish (bayildi means 'fainted'). Was it because of overindulgence, or his shock at the amount of olive oil that had been used in the dish by his wife? We will never know. In this version, however, the amount of oil used would not have caused the Imam any distress, although the sumptuousness of the result might still cause a swoon.

Try to use a slim variety of aubergine, long or short does not matter. This makes a good party dish as it tastes even better when left to stand for a few hours.

SERVES *4*

PREPARATION *30 minutes*

COOKING *about 1¼ hours*

Calories per serving *230*
Total fat *High*
Saturated fat *Low*
Protein *Low*
Carbohydrate *Low*
Cholesterol *Nil*
Vitamins *A, B₁, B₃, B₆, Folate, E*
Minerals *Potassium, Iron, Zinc*

4 AUBERGINES, TOTAL WEIGHT ABOUT 1 KG / 2¼ LB
4 TABLESPOONS OLIVE OIL
350 G / 12 OZ ONIONS, FINELY CHOPPED
5-6 GARLIC CLOVES, PEELED AND CRUSHED
500 G / 1 LB 2 OZ TOMATOES, FINELY CHOPPED
FEW SPRIGS OF FRESH THYME AND MARJORAM,
COARSELY CHOPPED, PLUS MORE FOR GARNISH
3-4 TABLESPOONS FINELY CHOPPED PARSLEY
1 RED SWEET PEPPER
2 TABLESPOONS TOMATO PASTE, DILUTED IN 300 ML / ½ PINT HOT WATER
SALT AND FRESHLY GROUND BLACK PEPPER

1 Preheat the oven to 190°C/375°F/gas 5 and lightly oil a baking sheet. If the aubergines still have their stalks on, try to keep them intact for decorative effect. Slit each aubergine lengthwise to open out like a pouch. Lay the aubergines on the baking sheet, slit side down. Brush a little oil on each aubergine and bake for 30 minutes. Take them out of the oven, but keep the oven on with the temperature reduced to 180°C/350°F/gas 4.
2 While the aubergines are baking, prepare the tomato sauce: put the onions in a frying pan with 3-4 tablespoons of water and bring to a simmer. Once the water has evaporated, add the remaining oil and sauté the onion until it is light gold. Add the garlic and stir for a few seconds. Then add the tomatoes and herbs, but keep a few sprigs of thyme and marjoram

for garnish. Season with salt and pepper and cook gently for 20 minutes, until the sauce looks well amalgamated and quite dry.
3 While the sauce is cooking, scorch the pepper over a naked flame for a few minutes. Peel it, cut it in half and deseed it. Then cut the flesh into long strips. Set these aside.
4 Arrange the aubergines side by side in a baking dish which is just large enough to hold them snugly in a single layer, this time with the slit side upwards. Sprinkle some salt and pepper over them and then fill each aubergine with the tomato sauce, distributing it evenly. Lay the pepper ribbons diagonally over the stuffing. Pour the diluted tomato paste into the bottom of the dish and bake for 45 minutes, basting the aubergines occasionally. Garnish with the reserved herbs.

Imam Bayildi

FENNEL GRATIN WITH OIL AND CHEESE

Finocchio – Florence fennel – is an undervalued vegetable with a cool elegant flavour. Although it is often served raw in salads and its refreshing effects are undoubted, occasionally it appears cooked in Italy and I am always freshly surprised by its finesse and its deliciousness. When cooked, its sweet taste and anise aromas are better projected if it is complemented by a softer texture. It makes an ideal partner for fish, particularly grilled fish.

SERVES *4*

PREPARATION *about 10 minutes*

COOKING *about 35 minutes*

Calories per serving *146*
Total fat *High*
Saturated fat *Medium*
Protein *Medium*
Carbohydrate *Low*
Cholesterol *8 mg*
Vitamins *B₁, B₆, Folate*
Minerals *Calcium, Potassium, Iron, Zinc*

4 FENNEL BULBS
2½ TABLESPOONS OLIVE OIL
3 TABLESPOONS FRESHLY GRATED PARMESAN CHEESE

1 TABLESPOON FENNEL SEEDS
¼ TEASPOON COARSE SEA SALT
2 TABLESPOONS TOASTED BREADCRUMBS

1 Preheat the oven to 190°C/375°F/gas 5 and lightly oil a small gratin dish. Slice off and discard the feathery tops of the fennel. Trim and discard the thick base. If the fennel is bruised or dried up, remove and discard its outer layer. Slice each bulb in two lengthwise.
2 Bring a saucepan of water to the boil, add the fennel pieces and boil them for 4-6 minutes, until they are softer but still with a little resistance in them. Drain them in a colander and then place them closely together in the prepared gratin dish.
3 Heat the remaining olive oil gently in a small frying pan, add the fennel seeds and swirl them around for 1 minute, until they start to sizzle. Dribble the oil and seeds over the fennel and then sprinkle the salt, cheese and breadcrumbs over the top, in that order.
4 Bake on the upper shelf of the oven for 20 minutes, until lightly brown on top.

BAKED AUBERGINES WITH MOZZARELLA

This is a very easy dish, loved by all. Its simplicity makes it the ideal standby. It is based on one served to us by my friend the writer Gillian Riley, who is an expert on Italian food. It can be served hot or at room temperature, with a salad and some interesting bread, such as ciabatta, or French baguette.

SERVES *4*

PREPARATION *20 minutes*

COOKING *25-35 minutes*

450 G / 1 LB AUBERGINES (2 MEDIUM AUBERGINES)
2 TABLESPOONS OLIVE OIL
1 TABLESPOON SUNFLOWER OIL
2 GARLIC CLOVES, PEELED AND CRUSHED
1 TEASPOON DRIED MARJORAM
½ TEASPOON DRIED THYME

SALT AND FRESHLY GROUND BLACK PEPPER

FOR THE TOPPING:
115 G / 4 OZ BUFFALO MOZZARELLA CHEESE, CUT INTO 1.5 CM / ½ IN DICE
225 G / 8 OZ TOMATOES, THINLY SLICED

1 Preheat the oven to 200°C/400°F/gas 6. Cut the aubergines into round slices about ½ cm / ¼ in thick. Mix the remaining ingredients in a bowl. Dip the slices of aubergine in the bowl, one at a time, to coat them lightly, and arrange them closely in a single layer in a large roasting pan. If you cannot fit them all in, cook them in 2 batches. Bake for 10 minutes.

2 Take the aubergines out of the oven and lower the oven setting to 190°C/375°F/gas 5. Top each aubergine slice with a slice of tomato and 3-4 Mozzarella pieces. Return to the oven and bake for 15 more minutes.

3 Take them out of the oven and immediately transfer them to a flat platter to prevent them absorbing any more oil.

Calories per serving *185*
Total fat *High*
Saturated fat *High*
Protein *Medium*
Carbohydrate *Low*
Cholesterol *19 mg*
Vitamins *A, B$_{12}$, C, E*
Minerals *Calcium, Potassium*

CAPONATA
Sicilian Aubergines in Sweet-and-sour Sauce

Sicilian caponata *bears the hallmarks of its Arab ancestry in its fusion of sweet and sour tastes. However, this fusion should be balanced so that the* caponata *does not lose its charm. Make sure it does not taste predominantly sour, so taste first and then add any extra vinegar if you wish. Traditionally the aubergines are first fried and then added to the dish. However, this version produces lighter results.*

900 KG / 2 LB AUBERGINES, DICED SMALL
3 TABLESPOONS OLIVE OIL
1 LARGE ONION, PEELED AND SLICED FINELY
1 TEASPOON DRIED OREGANO
2 YOUNG CELERY STALKS, CHOPPED
450 G / 1 LB TOMATOES, SKINNED AND CHOPPED, OR ONE 400 G / 14 OZ TIN OF CHOPPED TOMATOES

1 TEASPOON DEMERARA SUGAR
115 G / 4 OZ GREEN OLIVES, RINSED AND STONED
3 TABLESPOONS CAPERS, RINSED
2-3 TABLESPOONS RED WINE VINEGAR
2 TABLESPOONS PINE NUTS, TOASTED IN A DRY FRYING PAN
FRESHLY GROUND BLACK PEPPER

1 Heat the oil gently in a heavy-based saucepan and sauté the onion in it until light golden. Add the oregano and aubergines and keep turning them with a spatula for 5-10 minutes until they wilt a little.

2 Add the remaining ingredients except the pine nuts and only 2 tablespoons of the vinegar at this stage. Cover and simmer for 35-40 minutes, until everything is soft.

3 Taste and adjust the seasoning, adding more vinegar if necessary for a sweet-and-sour balance. Serve the caponata at room temperature, scattering the toasted nuts over it at the last minute.

SERVES *6*

PREPARATION
30 minutes

COOKING
45 minutes, plus cooling

Calories per serving *165*
Total fat *High*
Saturated fat *Low*
Protein *Low*
Carbohydrate *Low*
Cholesterol *Nil*
Vitamins *A, B$_1$, B$_3$, B$_6$, Folate, C, E*
Minerals *Potassium, Iron, Zinc*

FRESH PEAS AND COURGETTES

This is a simple vegetable dish, but when the vegetables are in season the combination can be astounding. The stars of the show are the peas and there is no alternative to freshly shelled. Choose young small courgettes, if you can find them, but you could use tiny carrots or small new potatoes instead. This dish can be prepared in advance – even the day before – and served at room temperature.

1.25 KG / 3 LB FRESH PEAS, SHELLED (SHELLED WEIGHT ABOUT 675 G / 1½ LB)
350 G / 12 OZ (IDEALLY SMALL) COURGETTES, INCLUDING THEIR FLOWERS IF STILL ATTACHED
6 SPRING ONIONS, COARSELY CHOPPED
3-4 TABLESPOONS FRUITY OLIVE OIL

225 G / 8 OZ (3-4) TOMATOES, SKINNED, DESEEDED AND DICED
150 ML / ¼ PINT (OR A LITTLE MORE) HOT WATER
2 TABLESPOONS FRESH DILL, COARSELY CHOPPED
SALT AND FRESHLY GROUND BLACK PEPPER

1 Keep the courgettes whole if small; if large, quarter them lengthwise.
2 Sauté the spring onions in the oil (reserving 1 tablespoon) until glistening, add the peas and tomatoes and stir for 2-3 minutes.
3 Add the water with seasoning. Cover and simmer for 10 minutes. Add the courgettes and more water if needed. All the vegetables should be submerged in the sauce. Cook gently for 30-35 minutes more, shaking the pan occasionally. Sprinkle in the dill and the remaining spring onions and cook for a few minutes more.
4 Turn out on a serving platter, dribble the last tablespoonful of oil all over and serve.

SERVES *4*

PREPARATION *30 minutes*

COOKING *about 1 hour*

Calories per serving *317*
Total fat *Medium*
Saturated fat *Medium*
Protein *Medium*
Carbohydrate *Low*
Cholesterol *Nil*
Vitamins *A, B1, B6, C, E, Folate*
Minerals *Calcium, Potassium, Iron, Zinc*

CATALAN SPINACH

This is a Moorish leftover in the Catalan culinary book, which can accompany poultry or meat dishes but may also be served as part of the larger mezze *table.*

900 G / 2 LB SPINACH, COARSELY CHOPPED
2 TABLESPOONS OLIVE OIL
3 TABLESPOONS TOASTED PINE NUTS

3 TABLESPOONS RAISINS, SOAKED IN WARM WATER FOR 10 MINUTES AND RINSED
SALT AND FRESHLY GROUND BLACK PEPPER

1 Place the spinach in a large saucepan over gentle heat and keep stirring so that it all comes in touch with the hot base and wilts. Add a little salt and, once the spinach looks wilted and it has exuded enough moisture, cover the saucepan and let it steam for 5-7 minutes until soft. Drain in a colander.
2 Heat the oil in the saucepan, add the drained spinach, pine nuts, raisins and some black pepper and sauté for 5 more minutes, stirring occasionally and keeping an eye on it. It should be dry but moist by the end.

SERVES *4*

PREPARATION *20 minutes*

COOKING *about 15 minutes*

Calories per serving *188*
Total fat *High*
Saturated fat *Low*
Protein *Medium*
Carbohydrate *Low*
Cholesterol *Nil*
Vitamins *A, B1, B2, B3, B6, Folate, C, E*
Minerals *Calcium, Iron, Zinc, Potassium*

Fresh Peas and Courgettes

GLOBE ARTICHOKES WITH FRESH BROAD BEANS

With the first rays of spring sun, the street markets in Greece present mounds of beautiful green artichokes. A little later on the elegant slim broad beans appear, to be followed by the young fresh peas. So inevitably these vegetables are bubbling away in different combinations in every home in the spring.

SERVES *4 as a main course, or 6 as a first course*

PREPARATION *about 40 minutes*

COOKING *about 1 hour*

Calories per serving *200*
Total fat *High*
Saturated fat *Low*
Protein *High*
Carbohydrate *Low*
Cholesterol *Nil*
Vitamins *A, B₃, B₆, Folate, E*
Minerals *Potassium, Iron, Zinc*

4-6 MEDIUM-SIZED GLOBE ARTICHOKES
1.5 KG / 3 LB FRESH BROAD BEANS IN THEIR PODS OR
500 G / 1 LB 2 OZ FROZEN BEANS, DEFROSTED
2 LEMONS
1 LARGE ONION, THINLY SLICED
4 TABLESPOONS OLIVE OIL

425 ML / ¾ PINT HOT WATER
4-5 SPRING ONIONS, CHOPPED
1 RED SWEET PEPPER, DESEEDED AND DICED
LARGE HANDFUL OF FRESH DILL, FINELY CHOPPED
SALT AND FRESHLY GROUND BLACK PEPPER

1 Shell the broad beans, discarding larger pods but keeping some of the smaller younger ones. Trim these all the way round as you would do with large green beans and then cut them in half. Immerse them in a bowl of water, rinse them carefully and drain them.

2 Prepare the artichokes by discarding three-quarters or more of their outer leaves until you have reached the tender inner ones. Cut the stem down, leaving about 5 cm / 2 in attached. Trim off the upper section of the leaves and discard, leaving a short collar round the heart of the artichoke. Cut the artichoke in half lengthwise. You will see in the middle a hairy choke which should be extracted with a stainless steel spoon or knife and discarded. Now trim the stem and the outer base of the artichoke of the hard dark green skin. Have ready a bowl of water with the juice of half a lemon in it and drop in each artichoke half as you finish it.

3 In a wide-based saucepan, sauté the onion (but not the spring onions) in the hot oil until glistening and add the broad beans. Stir for a few minutes and then add the juice from the remaining 1½ lemons and the hot water. Once it comes to the boil, add the artichoke halves and shake the saucepan to fit everything neatly in it. Add some salt and pepper, cover and cook gently for 25 minutes. (Do not stir the contents or you may break the artichokes.)

4 Turn the artichokes over carefully, add the spring onions, the pepper, dill and a little more water if needed. Rotate the saucepan and tilt it to distribute things evenly, cover and cook for another 20-25 minutes, until the beans and their pods are quite soft.

5 Serve with lovely fresh bread and a plate of fresh greenery, such as some of the reserved raw younger broad bean pods, some more spring onions, some rocket or sprigs of parsley, some dill or whatever is to hand.

Globe Artichokes with Fresh Broad Beans

OKRA WITH DRIED LIMES

Okra is loved all over the eastern Mediterranean and often cooked in casseroles, usually with meat or chicken. In Egypt, they add a number of spices to okra dishes and I have also added the dried limes (see page 19) which are a favourite ingredient in Iran and the Gulf countries. With their aromatic sourness, they contribute a deep note to the overall taste. They may be removed from the finished dish, but offer them to aficionados who like to suck them. If you can't find dried limes, some fresh lime juice will still give a delicious result.

This dish works well served with Tabbouleh (page 145), Tahinosalata (page 46) or Italian Baked Aubergines with Mozzarella cheese (page 114).

SERVES 4

PREPARATION
10 minutes

COOKING
about 1 hour

Calories per serving *184*
Total fat *Low*
Saturated fat *Low*
Protein *Medium*
Carbohydrate *Low*
Cholesterol *Nil*
Vitamins *A, B₁, B₆, C, E,*
Folate
Minerals *Calcium, Iron,*
Zinc, Potassium

1 KG / 2¼ LB OKRA

3 DRIED LIMES, OR 2 TABLESPOONS FRESH LIME JUICE

3 TABLESPOONS OLIVE OIL

1 LARGE ONION, FINELY CHOPPED

1-2 DRIED CHILLIES

3 GARLIC CLOVES, CHOPPED

1 TABLESPOON GROUND CORIANDER SEEDS

400 G / 14 OZ TINNED CHOPPED TOMATOES

HANDFUL OF FRESH CORIANDER LEAVES, COARSELY CHOPPED

SALT AND FRESHLY GROUND BLACK PEPPER

1 Trim off and discard the okra tops (see page 14), rinse the okra gently in cold water and drain.

2 Heat the oil in a large saucepan, add the onion and stir until light golden. Add the chillies, garlic and ground coriander and sauté for a minute or two.

3 Add the tomatoes with their liquid. Once the liquid starts to bubble, add the okra, limes or lime juice and seasoning. Shake the pan to distribute the ingredients evenly, Cover and cook gently for 30 minutes. If you are using the dried limes, press them with a wooden spoon from time to time to encourage them to give up their flavour.

4 Add the fresh coriander and cook for 10 minutes more.

Okra with Dried Limes

MOROCCAN STUFFED TOMATOES AND PEPPERS

The practice of stuffing vegetables originated in the Middle East and in Persia. The Ottomans were also very keen on them, but they must have found their way to North Africa via the Arabs and, although they are not as common there as in Middle Eastern countries and Greece, they are found occasionally in grand buffets in Morocco. In the Hotel Mamounia in Marrakech we have had an exotic version, which was quite sweet with the addition of dried fruit and redolent of the warm aromas of cinnamon. In Anatolia in Turkey, it is not only vegetables but also fruits such as quinces or apples that are stuffed. This is probably an influence from Persia. Also in Anatolia, instead of rice stuffings, they may contain cracked wheat and/or chickpeas. There are endless variations in stuffings, with or without meat.

Every summer we had delicious stuffed vegetables at home, made by my grandmother who had lived in Smyrna until 1922 when the expulsion of the Greeks took place. These looked like an exotic tapestry, arranged in their large roasting tin before being taken to the local baker where things were routinely baked, as households did not possess ovens at that time. We always had a selection of all the summer vegetables, which included not only tomatoes and green peppers but also courgettes and elongated purple aubergines. When you are embarking on the making of such a dish it is worth stuffing some extra vegetables – say, an extra tomato and a pepper – as they are so popular.

SERVES *4*

PREPARATION *about 1 hour*

COOKING *about 1 hour*

Calories per serving *685*
Total fat *High*
Saturated fat *Low*
Protein *Low*
Carbohydrate *Low*
Cholesterol *Nil*
Vitamins *A, B$_1$, B$_2$, B$_3$, B$_6$, Folate, C, E*
Minerals *Calcium, Iron, Zinc, Potassium*

4 LARGE TOMATOES

4 LARGE GREEN SWEET PEPPERS

½ TEASPOON SUGAR

2 TABLESPOONS TOASTED BREADCRUMBS (2 SLICES OF TOASTED BREAD PUT THROUGH A FOOD PROCESSOR)

SALT AND FRESHLY GROUND BLACK PEPPER

FOR THE STUFFING:

4 TABLESPOONS OLIVE OIL

2 LARGE ONIONS, THINLY SLICED

2 CM / ¾ IN PIECE OF FRESH GINGER, PEELED AND GRATED

¼ TEASPOON GROUND ALLSPICE (OR 4 GRAINS OF IT)

2 SMALL CINNAMON STICKS

115 G / 4 OZ LONG-GRAIN RICE, RINSED

225 G / 8 OZ DRIED APRICOTS, COARSELY CHOPPED

50 G / 2 OZ DATES, STONED AND CHOPPED (OPTIONAL)

JUICE OF ½ LEMON

150 ML / ¼ PINT HOT WATER

LARGE HANDFUL OF FRESH PARSLEY, FINELY CHOPPED

HANDFUL OF FRESH CORIANDER, CHOPPED

4-5 SPRIGS OF MINT, CHOPPED

50 G / 2 OZ PINE NUTS, TOASTED LIGHTLY

50 G / 2 OZ FLAKED ALMONDS, TOASTED LIGHTLY

2 TABLESPOONS CURRANTS, RINSED

FOR THE SAUCE:

225 G / 8 OZ TOMATOES, PEELED AND FINELY CHOPPED

2 TABLESPOONS OLIVE OIL

150 ML / ¼ PINT HOT WATER

1 Preheat the oven to 180°C/350°F/gas 4. Cut a round slice off the top (stem end) of each of the 4 large tomatoes and set aside. Do the same with the peppers. Scoop most of the tomato flesh out with a teaspoon, chop it finely and set aside. Place the tomatoes upside down for about 5 minutes to allow excess moisture to drain off. Keep all their juices. Trim and deseed the peppers.

2 Prepare the stuffing: heat the oil in a saucepan or large frying pan and sauté the onion until light golden. Add the ginger and spices and mix them in for 1-2 minutes, until aromatic. Add the strained rice and sauté for a few minutes until well coated in the oil and the spices. Add the reserved tomato flesh and juices, the dried fruit, lemon juice and hot water. Let it simmer for 5 minutes until most of the liquid is absorbed. Take from the heat, remove the cinnamon and mix in the remaining ingredients. Season.

3 Place the prepared tomatoes and peppers closely together, standing up side by side, in a small roasting tin. Sprinkle a pinch of sugar inside each tomato and fill them up loosely with the stuffing. Do not press it down, so that it has room to expand. Fill the peppers in the same way and seal the tomatoes and peppers with their respective tops.

4 Mix the sauce ingredients in a small bowl and pour over the top and around the vegetables. Cook in the oven for 50 minutes, basting the vegetables from time to time.

5 Turn the oven up to 200°C/400°F/gas 6, sprinkle the breadcrumbs on top and bake for 15-20 more minutes, until the top browns.

Overleaf: Moroccan Stuffed Tomatoes and Peppers and Dolmathes (page 126)

DOLMATHES
Stuffed Vine Leaves

Dolmathes *are among the best dishes in Greek cooking. These small parcels, filled with the aromas of the fields, represent the essence of spring with their captivating tastes.*

Under the name of thria *they have been a favourite in Greece for some time, approximately two thousand years.* Thria *in ancient Greek meant 'fig leaves', but at least by the fifth century BC it also meant a dish of stuffed fig leaves, as they were mentioned in Aristophanes'* Knights *and* The Frogs, *according to research done by classicist Andrew Dalby in London. Soon they discovered that vine leaves made a more tasty alternative. So by the fifth century AD the definition given by lexicographers is: 'Fig or vine leaves; also foodstuffs wrapped in these.' So much for historical continuity.*

This is a laborious dish to make, so try to enlist some help. In Greece it is often the result of a joint effort of extended families, friends and neighbours. Vine leaves are stuffed with various ingredients all over the Middle East and Turkey, but I think the best versions are made in Greece.

Fresh vine leaves – ideally young ones at the beginning of the season – obviously produce the best results. Alternatively one can buy packets of preserved ones. If you have access to a vine, you can freeze its leaves in season. Pile them up in groups of a dozen, roll them up, cover with cling film and place in the freezer. Let them thaw at room temperature for two hours before use. (See previous pages.)

MAKES *about 40*

PREPARATION
about 1 hour

COOKING
about 1 hour

Calories *30 each*
Total fat *High*
Saturated fat *Low*
Protein *Low*
Carbohydrate *Low*
Cholesterol *Nil*
Vitamins *A*
Minerals *Potassium, Iron*

225 G / 8 OZ VINE LEAVES (45-48)
DILL, TO SERVE
1-2 LEMONS, CUT INTO WEDGES, TO SERVE

FOR THE STUFFING:
150 G / 5 OZ LONG-GRAIN RICE, RINSED AND DRAINED
350 G / 12 OZ ONIONS, FINELY CHOPPED
3 TABLESPOONS PINE NUTS, TOASTED LIGHTLY IN A DRY FRYING PAN

2 TABLESPOONS SULTANAS OR RAISINS, RINSED (OPTIONAL)
4-5 TABLESPOONS FINELY CHOPPED FRESH DILL
4 TABLESPOONS FINELY CHOPPED PARSLEY
3 TABLESPOONS COARSELY CHOPPED FRESH MINT
JUICE OF 1 LEMON
4 TABLESPOONS OLIVE OIL
425 ML / ¾ PINT HOT WATER
SALT AND FRESHLY GROUND BLACK PEPPER

1 Rinse the vine leaves and blanch them in batches of 6-8 in a saucepan of lightly salted boiling water for 1 minute, or less if they are young. Take them out with a slotted spatula and drain. They should be just wilted and not cooked. If using preserved leaves – which are very salty – rinse them first and plunge them in a bowl of boiling water for 5 minutes. Take out and place in a bowl of cold water, then rinse them again and place in a strainer.

2 Mix all the stuffing ingredients together in a bowl. However, use only half of the oil and lemon juice at this stage.

3 Line the base of a wide saucepan or sauté pan with some of the vine leaves. Trim the stalks of the others and spread each vine leaf

on a plate, uneven side upwards. If the leaf is small take a teaspoon of stuffing, if large take a tablespoonful, and place it along the stem end of the leaf. Press the stuffing into an elongated sausage-like shape and fold the stem end of the leaf over it. Next, fold inwards the two edges of the leaf and roll tightly to the end into a small cigar shape. Squeeze the rolled package in your hand to get rid of excess moisture if they appear too wet.

4 Arrange them tightly in circles around the base of the pan, trapping their loose ends underneath. When one layer is formed sprinkle over a little more seasoning and start another layer on top. It is best not to have more than 3 layers, otherwise you get the bottom ones overcooked and squashed. Dribble the remaining oil and lemon juice all over and then place a small inverted plate on top to keep them in place while cooking.

5 Slowly pour in the hot water, cover and simmer for 50 minutes. Try one and if the rice is too crunchy cook a little longer.

6 The dolmathes are delicious served hot or cold. Arrange on a pretty platter, garnish with dill and surround with lemon wedges.

BROAD BEANS WITH CHARD

This earthy-flavoured Middle Eastern dish – usually made by my friend Sami Zubaida, one of the best cooks around – has an instant appeal for everyone round the table. The dish is infinitely better when made in the autumn with that summer's crop, before the beans hit middle age.

285 G / 10 OZ WHOLE DRIED BROAD BEANS, SOAKED OVERNIGHT
450 G / 1 LB SWISS CHARD, TRIMMED OF STALKS AND COARSELY CHOPPED
3 TABLESPOONS OLIVE OIL
1 TABLESPOON GROUND CUMIN
1 TEASPOON GROUND CORIANDER
JUICE OF 1-2 LEMONS, ACCORDING TO TASTE
SALT AND FRESHLY GROUND BLACK PEPPER

SERVES *4*

PREPARATION *10-15 minutes, plus overnight soaking*

COOKING *1¼-1¾ hours*

Calories per serving *271*
Total fat *Medium*
Saturated fat *Low*
Protein *High*
Carbohydrate *Low*
Cholesterol *Nil*
Vitamins *A, B₁, B₂, B₃, B₆, Folate, C*
Minerals *Calcium, Potassium, Iron, Zinc*

1 Rinse the beans, cover them with plenty of fresh water and boil them until quite tender. This could take between 1 and 1½ hours, according to their age. Discard any skins which come off in the process. Drain, reserving 2 cupfuls of the cooking liquid.

2 Heat the oil in a sauté pan, add the spices and swirl them around for a minute until their aroma rises. Add the chard and sauté, turning it around with a spatula. Add half of the reserved cooking liquid with some seasoning. Cover and simmer gently for about 10-15 minutes, until soft.

3 Place the drained beans in a large bowl, add the cooked Swiss chard with some more seasoning and the lemon juice and toss to mix everything. It should be quite moist, almost soupy, so add a little more of the reserved cooking liquid if necessary.

4 Bowls of black olives, little plates of flat-leaved parsley on the stalk and rocket, and little scarlet radishes go well with this dish.

PUY LENTILS WITH DILL, SALSA VERDE AND ROAST PEPPERS

Puy lentils are the aristocrats among lentils. They are small, with a silvery-green coat and light green insides. However small and insignificant they may look, once cooked they hold their shape better than other lentils and their flavour is high up on the culinary scale. Of course not all Puy lentils in the market are the genuine article; that is they don't necessarily come from the town of Le Puy in the Auvergne. A lot are Puy-style lentils grown elsewhere in France or in other European countries, but they are still better than the large green lentils, which are tasteless and disintegrate easily. This is the most delicious lentil recipe and it has evolved after numerous trials.

SERVES *4 people as a main course, or 6 as a first course*

PREPARATION *about 20 minutes, plus cooling*

COOKING *40-50 minutes*

Calories per serving *376*
Total fat *Low*
Saturated fat *Low*
Protein *High*
Carbohydrate *Medium*
Cholesterol *Nil*
Vitamins *A, B₁, B₂, B₃, B₆, Folate, C, E*
Minerals *Calcium, Potassium, Iron, Zinc, Selenium*

4 RED SWEET PEPPERS, RINSED AND DRIED
450 G / 1 LB PUY OR SIMILAR SMALL LENTILS, PICKED CLEAN AND RINSED
LARGE HANDFUL OF FRESH DILL, COARSELY CHOPPED
SALT AND FRESHLY GROUND BLACK PEPPER

FOR THE SALSA VERDE:
2 FRESH GREEN CHILLIES, DESEEDED AND CHOPPED
3 GARLIC CLOVES, PEELED AND CHOPPED
1.5 CM / ½ IN PIECE OF FRESH GINGER, PEELED AND GRATED
LARGE HANDFUL OF FLAT-LEAVED PARSLEY, CHOPPED
SMALL HANDFUL OF FRESH DILL, CHOPPED
1 TEASPOON DIJON MUSTARD
JUICE OF 1½ LEMONS
3 TABLESPOONS OLIVE OIL

1 Preheat the oven to 190°C/375°F/gas 5. Cover a baking sheet with foil, lay the peppers on it and roast them for 35-40 minutes, turning them over once about halfway through. Remove them from the oven and when they are cool enough to handle, peel them, trim them and deseed them. Keep one pepper aside for the salsa and cut the rest into small dice.

2 Cover the lentils with cold water, bring to the boil and drain. Cover them with fresh water, bring to the boil and simmer very briefly, keeping an eye on them. They will take about 7-9 minutes, as they must still be a little hard. Drain them and empty them into a large bowl. Add some seasoning, the diced peppers, the dill and mix well.

3 To make the salsa, place all the ingredients apart from the oil in a food processor, add the reserved roast pepper and process with short bursts until everything has the consistency of crumbs. With the machine still running, add the olive oil, dribbling it in slowly until it all looks well amalgamated.

4 A couple of hours before they are to be served, coat the lentils with this salsa so that all the exotic flavours have a chance to permeate the lentils. Garnish with some reserved dill and parsley sprigs.

Puy Lentils with Dill, Salsa Verde and Roast Peppers

CHICKPEA AND SPINACH CASSEROLE

On the whole, chickpeas are neglected in the West; not so in the Middle East, where they appear transformed in a hundred guises. There is no mezze *table without the sharply appetizing* hummus *of the Arab countries and Turkey, and in most of the Mediterranean countries chickpeas are also made into wonderful casseroles and soups – in combination with spices, vegetables or meat.*

This recipe was described to me first in the middle 1960s by a Cypriot shoemaker in North London's Chapel Market, and an almost identical one is made all over Cyprus using black-eyed beans.

SERVES *4-6 as a main course*

PREPARATION
20 minutes, plus overnight soaking

COOKING
about 2¼ hours

Calories per serving *354*
Total fat *Medium*
Saturated fat *Low*
Protein *Medium*
Carbohydrate *Low*
Cholesterol *Nil*
Vitamins *A, B₁, B₂, B₃, B₆, Folate, C, E*
Minerals *Calcium, Potassium, Iron, Zinc*

350 G / 12 OZ CHICKPEAS, PICKED CLEAN AND SOAKED OVERNIGHT IN COLD WATER

450 G / 1 LB FRESH SPINACH, OR 285 G / 10 OZ PACKET OF FROZEN LEAF SPINACH, DEFROSTED

2 LARGE ONIONS, CHOPPED

4 TABLESPOONS OLIVE OIL

1-2 TABLESPOONS GROUND CUMIN

4-5 GARLIC CLOVES, CHOPPED

1 LEMON

SALT AND FRESHLY GROUND BLACK PEPPER

1 Drain and rinse the chickpeas. In a large pan, cover with plenty of fresh water and bring to the boil. Skim, cover and cook until they are soft. This could take about 1 hour or more (if using a pressure cooker, about 20 minutes). Strain, but keep the liquid.

2 Using the same saucepan, sauté the onions in the hot oil until glistening and add the cumin and the garlic. When they become aromatic, add the chickpeas and enough of their cooking liquid barely to cover them. Add the lemon juice, cover and simmer for about 1 hour.

3 Towards the end of that time, if using fresh spinach rinse it, drain and chop it coarsely. Add the spinach, salt and a generous amount of pepper to the casserole. Mix well and cook for a further 15-20 minutes, or a little less if using frozen.

4 This dish actually improves with standing so it can be cooked the day before. It may also be served at room temperature. Serve it with Sarimsakli Yoghurt, the garlicky Turkish yoghurt sauce (page 33).

Top: Chickpea and Spinach Casserole; bottom: Fava (page 132)

MAGHREBI LENTILS WITH CHERMOULA

Lentils can be transformed from the humble ingredient they are to royal status with the addition of a few aromatic ingredients. With their nutty flavour accentuated with garlic, spices and herbs – and given the speed with which they can be prepared – they make the most delicious standby dishes. In Morocco, chermoula *sauce is often used as a marinade for fish. This dish can be served with any grilled meats or fish, or by itself with Turkish Muhammara (page 42) or Tahinosalata (page 46) and fresh bread.*

SERVES *4*

PREPARATION *20 minutes*

COOKING *about 20 minutes, plus cooling*

Calories per serving *301*
Total fat *Medium*
Saturated fat *Low*
Protein *High*
Carbohydrate *Low*
Cholesterol *Nil*
Vitamins *A, B₁, B₂, B₃, B₆, Folate, C*
Minerals *Iron, Zinc, Selenium, Potassium*

285 G / 10 OZ SMALL BROWN-GREEN LENTILS, RINSED

2 BAY LEAVES

FOR THE CHERMOULA SAUCE:
3 TABLESPOONS OLIVE OIL
1 FRESH CHILLI, DESEEDED AND FINELY CHOPPED
1 TABLESPOON GROUND CUMIN
1 TABLESPOON PAPRIKA

1 TEASPOON GROUND CORIANDER
¼ TEASPOON GROUND CINNAMON
3 GARLIC CLOVES, PEELED AND CRUSHED
4 TABLESPOONS EACH COARSELY CHOPPED CORIANDER AND FLAT-LEAVED PARSLEY
3 TABLESPOONS FRESH MINT, FINELY CHOPPED
JUICE OF 1 OR 2 LEMONS
SALT AND FRESHLY GROUND BLACK PEPPER

1 Rinse the lentils, cover with fresh water, add the bay leaves and bring to the boil. Simmer gently for 15-20 minutes. The lentils should be soft enough to eat, but still intact and a little firm. Drain and discard the bay leaves.
2 Make the sauce: heat the oil gently in a sauté pan and sauté the chilli and spices briefly for about 1 minute. Add the garlic and, as soon as it becomes aromatic, add the lentils and stir to coat them in the sauce. Add the herbs and some seasoning, stir for a further minute and then withdraw from the heat.
3 Let the mixture cool a little before serving. Add the juice of 1 lemon first, taste and adjust accordingly (it should be quite sharp-tasting). Serve either warm or at room temperature.

FAVA
Yellow Split Pea Purée

SERVES *4*

PREPARATION *about 20 minutes, plus 1 hour's soaking*

COOKING *about 1 hour*

If you ask any Greek, they will tell you that fava *is the dish that sustained them in the frugal years after the War. However,* fava *goes back even longer than that – perhaps a couple of thousand years – as it is the kind of dish which was popular in Classical Greece. A very similar-sounding dish called* etnos *was sold in the streets of Athens and, according to Aristophanes, it was a favourite of Hercules. Although neglected during the affluent 1970s and 1980s, it has made a triumphant return, acknowledged as one of those dishes which make up the basic fabric of healthy Mediterranean food. Greek* fava *are smaller than ordinary yellow split peas, have a sweeter taste and are not as solid. (See previous page.)*

225 G / 8 OZ GREEK FAVA, OR 150 G / 5 OZ YELLOW
SPLIT PEAS

1 SMALL ONION, FINELY CHOPPED

2-3 SMALL RED ONIONS, THINLY SLICED

2-3 TABLESPOONS OLIVE OIL

JUICE OF 1 LEMON

1 TABLESPOON CHOPPED PARSLEY

4-5 BLACK OLIVES

SALT AND FRESHLY GROUND BLACK PEPPER

1 LEMON, QUARTERED, TO SERVE

Calories per serving *197*
Total fat *Medium*
Saturated fat *Low*
Protein *Medium*
Carbohydrate *Low*
Cholesterol *Nil*
Vitamins B$_1$, B$_3$, Folate, E
Minerals *Iron, Zinc, Potassium*

1 Pick the peas clean from grit and soak them in cold water for about 1 hour. Rinse them several times, place in a heavy-based pan and add 1 litre / 1¾ pints of water. Bring to the boil and skim until clear.

2 Add the onion and simmer, uncovered, for 45-50 minutes, stirring occasionally. Add salt towards the end of cooking time. When the split peas appear mushy towards the end, keep an eye on them as they may stick. Taste them to make sure they are properly cooked; if not,

add a little extra water. Once cooked, the mixture should look soupy.

3 Mash it properly with a potato masher or put it through a food processor immediately, while it is still hot, as it solidifies once cold.

4 Spread the purée on a platter before it solidifies and let it cool. Sprinkle the red onions all over the top, followed by some black pepper, olive oil, lemon juice and chopped parsley. Pile the olives in the centre and serve warm or cold with lemon wedges.

MAS PIYAZI
Mung Bean Salad with Fresh Pomegranates

This Turkish dish can also be made with Puy or small brown lentils instead of mung beans.

225 G / 8 OZ MUNG BEANS, PICKED CLEAN AND
SOAKED FOR 2 HOURS

2 POMEGRANATES, PEELED AND SEEDS EXTRACTED
RESERVING ANY JUICES (SEE PAGE 19)

3 SMALL RED ONIONS OR SHALLOTS, THINLY SLICED

3 SPRING ONIONS, THINLY SLICED

LARGE HANDFUL OF FLAT-LEAVED PARSLEY, FINELY
CHOPPED

LARGE HANDFUL OF ROCKET, COARSELY CHOPPED

1 TABLESPOON ANTEP PEPPER (PAGE 15) OR RED
PEPPER FLAKES

FOR THE DRESSING:

5 TABLESPOONS POMEGRANATE SYRUP, DILUTED IN 5
TABLESPOONS WATER, OR THE JUICE OF 1 LEMON

3 TABLESPOONS LIGHT OLIVE OIL OR GROUNDNUT OIL

SERVES *4-6*

PREPARATION *25 minutes, plus 2 hours' soaking*

COOKING *25 minutes*

Calories per serving *242*
Total fat *Medium*
Saturated fat *Low*
Protein *High*
Carbohydrate *Medium*
Cholesterol *Nil*
Vitamins A, B$_1$, B$_3$, B$_6$, Folate, C
Minerals *Potassium, Iron, Zinc*

1 Drain and rinse the mung beans. Cover with fresh water and boil gently until they are tender but not disintegrating (which happens suddenly and rapidly), about 25 minutes. (Lentils will take 10 minutes.)

2 Drain and mix with the remaining

ingredients. Season with salt to taste.

3 Mix the dressing ingredients together, including the reserved pomegranate juices. (If the syrup is too set to pour out, sit the bottle in hot water for 15 minutes.) Pour over the beans and toss gently until well mixed.

Salads

SALADE NIÇOISE

This is a dish with a double identity, like Dr Jekyll and Mr Hyde. It can be sensational and it can also be an amalgam of tired leftovers. Every family restaurant in Nice will have a different version of it, all claiming theirs is the most authentic. In my mind there are certain things that have to be included to call it a true salade niçoise. The basics are potatoes (ideally small or new and tasty), tuna (ideally fresh but tinned will do), French green beans, tomatoes, tinned anchovy fillets, olives and, maybe, lettuce. The potatoes respond much better to vinaigrette if they are dressed while they are still hot.

SERVES *4*

PREPARATION *25 minutes*

COOKING *12-15 minutes*

Calories per serving *419*
Total fat *High*
Saturated fat *Low*
Protein *High*
Carbohydrate *Low*
Cholesterol *170 mg*
Vitamins *A, B group, C, E*
Minerals *Calcium, Potassium, Iron, Zinc, Selenium, Iodine*

550 G / 1¼ LB SMALL POTATOES, RINSED

225 G / 8 OZ FRENCH GREEN BEANS, TOPPED, TAILED AND STEAMED UNTIL JUST TENDER

1 RED SWEET PEPPER, TRIMMED, DESEEDED AND SLICED INTO THIN STRIPS

200 G / 7 OZ TIN OF TUNA IN SUNFLOWER OIL, DRAINED

285 G / 10 OZ TOMATOES, TRIMMED AND CUT INTO THIN WEDGES

1 LARGE RED ONION, THINLY SLICED

4 TINNED ANCHOVY FILLETS, DRAINED AND FINELY CHOPPED

3 TABLESPOONS CAPERS, RINSED AND DRAINED

HANDFUL OF FLAT-LEAVED PARSLEY, FINELY CHOPPED

2-3 SPRIGS OF BASIL, TORN BY HAND

6-8 SMALL BLACK OLIVES

5-6 SMALL CRISP COS LETTUCE LEAVES (OPTIONAL)

3 HARD-BOILED EGGS, SHELLED AND QUARTERED

FOR THE VINAIGRETTE:

3 TABLESPOONS OLIVE OIL

2 TABLESPOONS RED WINE VINEGAR

1 TEASPOON COARSE-GRAIN FRENCH MUSTARD

2 TABLESPOONS LIGHT FROMAGE FRAIS

SALT AND FRESHLY GROUND BLACK PEPPER

1 Boil the potatoes in their skins, making sure they are not overcooked. Drain and, when cool enough to handle, peel them. If they are small, cut them in half lengthwise; if they are larger, cut them into small walnut-sized pieces. Place the potatoes in a large bowl.

2 Beat the vinaigrette ingredients together until smooth, taste and adjust the seasoning if necessary. Coat the potatoes with it while they are still warm. These can now wait for a few hours, if necessary, covered with film.

3 Just before the salad is to be served, add to the bowl the remaining ingredients, except the lettuce, if using, and the eggs. Toss gently to coat everything in the vinaigrette.

4 If you are using lettuce, arrange the leaves on a platter and empty the salad on them. Otherwise, just tip the salad directly on to the platter. Garnish with the hard-boiled egg quarters.

Salade Niçoise

FATTOUSH
Bread and Purslane Salad

This Syrian salad is loved all around the Eastern Mediterranean coast. Bread, particularly stale bread, has always been used ingeniously in Mediterranean countries. The Italian panzanella *is a salad not unlike* fattoush. *Often the bread is toasted and used with soups like the Castilian* sopa de ajo *or the Egyptian* fata. *This variation comes from my friend Sami Zubaida – one of the many treats we have had round his large table. The dark red flakes of sumak are a must for the authentic slightly sour tone of the salad.*

SERVES *4*

PREPARATION *25-30 minutes, at least 1 hour before serving*

Calories per serving *211*
Total fat *Medium*
Saturated fat *Low*
Protein *Low*
Carbohydrate *Low*
Cholesterol *Nil*
Vitamins *A, B₁, B₃, B₆, Folate, C, E*
Minerals *Calcium, Potassium, Iron*

2 PITTA BREADS OR 3 SLICES OF STALE WHITE BREAD
SMALL BUNCH OF PURSLANE OR ROCKET
1 SMALL GREEN SWEET PEPPER
1 SMALL CUCUMBER, RINSED AND FINELY DICED
4-5 SMALL TOMATOES, QUARTERED
3-4 SPRING ONIONS, CHOPPED
LARGE HANDFUL OF PARSLEY, FINELY CHOPPED
2 TABLESPOONS FINELY CHOPPED FRESH CORIANDER

3 TABLESPOONS FINELY CHOPPED FRESH MINT
1 TABLESPOON SUMAK FLAKES (OPTIONAL)

FOR THE VINAIGRETTE:
JUICE OF 1-2 LEMONS
3 TABLESPOONS OLIVE OIL
2 GARLIC CLOVES, PEELED AND CRUSHED
SALT AND FRESHLY GROUND BLACK PEPPER

1 Toast the bread until crisp and then break it up into small uneven pieces.
2 Trim the purslane or rocket of its thick stalks and coarsely chop the leaves. Trim and deseed the pepper, and cut it into small dice. Place all the salad ingredients in a large bowl.
3 Beat the vinaigrette ingredients together and season. Add this to the bowl and toss the salad

to coat everything in the dressing. The moisture from the vegetables and the herbs will help moisten the bread (the original recipe uses much more oil, so feel free to add more if you are not counting calories). However, the dressing is best added at least 1 hour before serving, so that the bread softens and absorbs all the other flavours.

HORIATIKI SALATA

SERVES *4*

PREPARATION *15-20 minutes*

Calories per serving *177*
Total fat *High*
Saturated fat *High*
Protein *Low*

Horiatiki, *meaning simply 'peasant style', is a salad now synonymous with Greek summer meals, usually as a prelude to grilled fish or souvlaki. It is also substantial enough to make lunch by itself.*

285 G / 10 OZ RIPE TOMATOES
1 MEDIUM RED ONION, QUARTERED
½ GREEN SWEET PEPPER, DESEEDED AND SLICED THINLY IN RIBBONS
SMALL PIECE OF CUCUMBER, THINLY SLICED

6-8 BLACK OLIVES
115 G / 4 OZ GREEK FETA CHEESE, SLICED INTO 4
¼ TEASPOON DRIED OREGANO
3 TABLESPOONS OLIVE OIL
SALT AND FRESHLY GROUND PEPPER

1 Slice the tomatoes in half and trim off the stalk ends. Slice each half into thick wedges. Slice each onion quarter very thinly.

2 Place all the ingredients, apart from the cheese, oregano and 1 teaspoon of the olive oil, in a bowl. Season to taste and toss gently to mix everything and coat it in the oil.

3 Place the slices of Feta on top, drizzle the reserved oil on it and sprinkle the oregano all over. You now have an authentic horiatiki.

Carbohydrate *Low*
Cholesterol *20 mg*
Vitamins *A, B group, C, E*
Minerals *Calcium, Potassium*

MESCLUN WITH GOATS' CHEESE

It is only in France and Italy that I have come across a proper mixture of salad greens to deserve the name of the original Provençal mesclun. *The best way to form an idea of what it can be is to visit one of the large Mediterranean markets, such as that in Nice or the Mercato Centrale near the Piazza San Lorenzo in Florence, where the selection is particularly astounding in the autumn.*

A mesclun *should include young leaves of both wild and cultivated greens, such as dandelion,* barba di cappuccino *(monk's beard), tiny peppery rocket leaves, lamb's lettuce, purslane, chervil, oak-leaf lettuce and occasionally a number of unrecognizable items seasonal and indigenous to the area. Such items are often sold already mixed as well as separately. Very rarely do we have access to such a glowing array of crisply fresh greenery, but we can improvise. Try to use the crisp inner leaves of different lettuce hearts for the basis of the salad. Rocket leaves are indispensable.*

175 G / 6 OZ MESCLUN OR A VARIETY OF SALAD LEAVES AND HERBS AS ABOVE

85 G / 3 OZ MATURE OR SEMI-MATURE GOATS' CHEESE WITH A SHARP TASTE AND CRUMBLY TEXTURE, SUCH AS A CROTTIN

FOR THE VINAIGRETTE:

1 TABLESPOON BALSAMIC VINEGAR

1 TABLESPOON LEMON JUICE

1 SMALL GARLIC CLOVE, CRUSHED

2 TABLESPOONS HAZELNUT OR WALNUT OIL

SALT

SERVES *4*

PREPARATION *10-15 minutes*

Calories per serving *109*
Total fat *Medium*
Saturated fat *Medium*
Protein *Medium*
Carbohydrate *Low*
Cholesterol *20 mg*
Vitamins *B₁₂, Folate*
Minerals *Calcium, Potassium*

1 Place the mixed salad leaves in a bowl and crumble the cheese on top.

2 Beat together all the vinaigrette ingredients, apart from the oil. Then beat in the oil and adjust the seasoning, if necessary. Pour the dressing over the salad and toss well.

Overleaf left to right: Mesclun with Goats' Cheese, Black Olive Salad with Pimentón (page 142), Mozzarella with Sun-Dried Tomatoes, Anchovy and Basil (page 142)

MOZZARELLA WITH SUN-DRIED TOMATOES, ANCHOVY AND BASIL

This easy dish of strong simple flavours makes an ideal standby. (See previous pages.)

SERVES *4*

PREPARATION *10 minutes*

Calories per serving *299*
Total fat *High*
Saturated fat *Medium*
Protein *Low*
Carbohydrate *Low*
Cholesterol *Nil*
Vitamins *B₃, B₁₂, E*
Minerals *Potassium, Iron, Iodine*

1 BUFFALO MOZZARELLA CHEESE, ABOUT 140 G / 5 OZ
6 PIECES OF SUN-DRIED TOMATOES PRESERVED IN OIL
SMALL HANDFUL OF BASIL LEAVES
3 TINNED ANCHOVY FILLETS, CUT INTO 3-4 PIECES

12 BLACK OLIVES
2 TABLESPOONS OLIVE OIL
1 TEASPOON BALSAMIC VINEGAR

1 Slice the Mozzarella thinly and arrange the pieces on a pretty platter. Top each slice with a sun-dried tomato, and then with 1 or 2 small pieces of anchovy. Sprinkle the olives all over.
2 Beat the oil and vinegar lightly and sprinkle this all over the salad. Decorate with the basil leaves and serve.

BLACK OLIVE SALAD WITH PIMENTÓN

This is a salad which appears both in Spain – often as tapas *– and in North Africa. It goes well with grilled kebabs and fish, as well as pulse dishes, such as the Broad Beans with Swiss Chard (page 127) or Chickpea and Spinach Casserole (page 130). (See previous pages.)*

SERVES *4*

PREPARATION *15-20 minutes, plus 1-2 hours' standing*

Calories per serving *140*
Total fat *High*
Saturated fat *Medium*
Protein *Low*
Carbohydrate *Low*
Cholesterol *Nil*
Vitamins *A, C, E*
Minerals *Potassium, Iron*

285 G / 10 OZ BLACK OLIVES, PITTED AND CHOPPED
1 TABLESPOON SWEET PIMENTÓN (PIMENTÓN DULCE, SEE PAGE 14) OR PAPRIKA
2 PURPLE SHALLOTS, OR 1 SMALL RED ONION
2 TABLESPOONS FINELY CHOPPED PARSLEY
1 LEMON, TO SERVE

FOR THE VINAIGRETTE:
JUICE OF ½ LEMON
1 GARLIC CLOVE, PEELED AND CRUSHED
¼ TEASPOON CUMIN
LARGE PINCH OF CHILLI POWDER
2 TABLESPOONS OLIVE OIL

1 Dice or thinly slice the shallots or onions. Place the salad ingredients in a bowl.
2 Beat together lightly all the vinaigrette ingredients, apart from the olive oil. Then beat in the oil gradually.
3 Pour the vinaigrette over the salad and toss to coat everything. Let the salad stand for 1-2 hours so that all the flavours can blend.
4 Empty the salad out on a platter and serve with lemon quarters and garnished with some reserved parsley sprigs. In hot weather it is best served lightly chilled.

COS LETTUCE WITH ROCKET AND DILL

This is the salad that I always return to when I am longing for a pure and refreshing taste. It is a salad with no frills, an everyday affair which we commonly had at home in Athens and which I find intimately familiar. Try to use the inner young leaves of the lettuce only, which taste sweeter.

1 COS LETTUCE
LARGE HANDFUL OF YOUNG ROCKET LEAVES
3 TABLESPOONS FINELY CHOPPED DILL
5 CM / 2 IN PIECE OF CUCUMBER, THINLY SLICED

2 SPRING ONIONS, THINLY SLICED
3 TABLESPOONS OLIVE OIL
1-2 TABLESPOONS LEMON JUICE
SALT

SERVES *4*

PREPARATION *15-20 minutes*

Calories per serving *95*
Total fat *High*
Saturated fat *Medium*
Protein *Low*
Carbohydrate *Low*
Cholesterol *Nil*
Vitamins *Folate, C, E*
Minerals *Potassium, Iron*

1 Trim and discard the outer leaves of the lettuce. Rinse the remaining leaves and dry them well. Place 3-4 leaves on top of each other, roll them together lengthwise and cut the roll across in thin slices, like a chiffonnade. Place the shreds in a bowl.
2 Chop the rocket leaves coarsely and add this to the lettuce, together with the spring onions and cucumber.
3 Beat the oil and lemon juice together lightly, pour this dressing over the salad and toss gently to coat everything in it.
4 Sprinkle the dill over the salad, followed by a little salt and toss a little more to mix in.

GREEN OLIVE AND POMEGRANATE SALAD

Of the thirty or so dishes that made the sumptuous lunch for us prepared and presented by the ladies of Gaziantep in south-east Turkey, this was the one that impressed me most with its simplicity and novelty. It is obviously a dish of autumn, when the scarlet pomegranates appear unabashedly in mountainous heaps on carts all over Turkey. This is also the time for the fresh crop of juicy green olives and the new tasty walnuts... all ingredients with sensational flavour.

225 G / 8 OZ GREEN OLIVES, STONED AND CHOPPED
2-3 SPRING ONIONS, FINELY CHOPPED
115 G / 4 OZ WALNUT PIECES
3-4 STALKS OF FLAT-LEAVED PARSLEY, FINELY CHOPPED

SEEDS AND JUICE FROM 1 POMEGRANATE (SEE PAGE 19)
3 TABLESPOONS OLIVE OIL
½ TEASPOON URFA PEPPER FLAKES (SEE PAGE 15) OR CHILLI FLAKES

SERVES *4*

PREPARATION *15-20 minutes*

COOKING *10 minutes*

Calories per serving *352*
Total fat *High*
Saturated fat *Low*
Protein *Low*
Carbohydrate *Low*
Cholesterol *Nil*
Vitamins *Folate, E*
Minerals *Iron, Zinc, Potassium, Calcium*

1 Preheat the oven to 160°C/325°F/gas 3. Line a baking tray with foil and spread the walnuts on it. Bake for 10 minutes. Take out and let the nuts cool, then chop them coarsely in a food processor or bash them with a rolling pin.
2 In a large bowl, combine the chopped nuts with all the other ingredients except the pepper flakes. Mix gently.
3 Spread the salad on a small platter and sprinkle the pepper flakes on top.

TABBOULEH
Lebanese Parsley Salad

When we have tabbouleh in the summer in Greece, my teenage daughter Alexandra complains because she says it is like eating the undergrowth of the surrounding hillsides or the garden… and this is exactly what tabbouleh is. A platter of it is like a synthesis of a kitchen garden, with its aromas, its colours, its different textures and its multi-layered tastes. A precious Eastern tapestry, which will revive you in the middle of a hot day like a panacea. Of course, one can improvise even with this classic dish: other herbs could be added, such as basil, dill or chopped rocket leaves.

200 G / 7 OZ BUNCH OF FLAT-LEAF PARSLEY, TRIMMED OF THICK STALKS

85 G / 3 OZ BULGAR (COARSE CRACKED WHEAT), PICKED OVER

4 TABLESPOONS FINELY CHOPPED FRESH MINT

7.5 CM / 3 IN PIECE OF CUCUMBER, PEELED AND DICED

3 SHALLOTS OR 1 MEDIUM RED ONION, DICED

3 SPRING ONIONS, FINELY CHOPPED

3 SMALL TOMATOES (ABOUT 200 G / 7 OZ), PEELED AND DICED

½ GREEN OR RED SWEET PEPPER, DICED

FOR THE VINAIGRETTE:

JUICE OF 1½-2 LEMONS

3 TABLESPOONS OLIVE OIL

SALT AND FRESHLY GROUND BLACK PEPPER

SERVES 4-6

PREPARATION *about 30 minutes, plus 30 minutes' soaking and 30 minutes' marinating*

Calories per serving *153*
Total fat *High*
Saturated fat *Low*
Protein *Low*
Carbohydrate *Low*
Cholesterol *Nil*
Vitamins A, B₁, B₃, *Folate, C, E*
Minerals *Calcium, Potassium, Iron*

1 Rinse the bulgar and soak in hot water for 20 minutes. Drain well and roll it in a kitchen towel in order to get rid of excess moisture. Place it in a bowl.

2 Chop the parsley by hand, not too finely but not coarsely either – it should have some texture in it and should not be a liquidized green mush. Add it to the bowl with all the other ingredients and mix everything together. Cover and chill lightly. *NOT vinaigrette*

3 Half an hour before serving, beat together the lemon juice with seasoning to taste. Then add the oil and beat until smooth.

4 Pour the dressing over the salad and toss well in order to coat everything in it. Taste and adjust the seasoning and add some more lemon juice if necessary.

5 Turn out on a platter to serve. The predominant colour of the salad should be green.

Tabbouleh

MOROCCAN ORANGE, CARROT, OLIVE AND CHICORY SALAD

Golden oranges play a part at every Moroccan table, as part of a salad or as a garnish. Where there are oranges, there is also the warming aroma of cinnamon. In medieval Arab cooking, cinnamon was used in both savoury and sweet dishes.

SERVES *4-6*

PREPARATION *15-20 minutes*

Calories per serving *80*
Total fat *Medium*
Saturated fat *Low*
Protein *Low*
Carbohydrate *High*
Cholesterol *Nil*
Vitamins *A, C, E, Folate*
Minerals *Iron, Potassium*

2 LARGE NAVEL ORANGES
175 G / 6 OZ CARROTS
8-10 GREEN OLIVES, STONED AND QUARTERED
1 HEAD OF CHICORY, TRIMMED
2 TABLESPOONS LIGHTLY TOASTED PINE NUTS
PINCH OF GROUND CINNAMON, TO GARNISH

FOR THE DRESSING:
2 TABLESPOONS LEMON JUICE
5-6 TABLESPOONS ORANGE JUICE
1 TABLESPOON CLEAR HONEY
2 TEASPOONS ORANGE FLOWER WATER
½ TEASPOON GROUND CINNAMON

1 Peel the oranges, removing as much white pith as you can. Slice the fruit horizontally into very thin rounds. Cover and chill.

2 Peel the carrots and pare into long shreds or grate them. Place the carrots and the quartered olives in a salad bowl.

3 Beat the dressing ingredients together until they are well blended. Reserving two tablespoonfuls, pour the dressing over the carrots and olives and toss until well coated.

4 Arrange the orange slices on a round platter. Pull the chicory leaves apart and place them around the orange. Scatter the carrots over the salad and sprinkle the pine nuts and a pinch of cinnamon on top. Finally, dribble the reserved dressing over the chicory and serve.

ORANGE, OLIVE AND ROCKET SALAD

This is an unorthodox treatment of the exotic salads from Morocco with a sweet-and-sour taste.

SERVES *4*

PREPARATION *15-20 minutes, plus chilling*

Calories per serving *154*
Total fat *High*
Saturated fat *Low*
Protein *Low*
Carbohydrate *Low*
Cholesterol *Nil*
Vitamins *B₁, B₆, Folate, C, E*
Minerals *Potassium, Zinc*

3 LARGE ORANGES, PEELED AND THINLY SLICED
115 G / 4 OZ BLACK OLIVES, HALVED AND STONED
LARGE HANDFUL OF ROCKET LEAVES OR WATERCRESS
3 TABLESPOONS FINELY CHOPPED PARSLEY OR CHERVIL

FOR THE VINAIGRETTE:
2 TABLESPOONS HAZELNUT OR WALNUT OIL
JUICE OF 1 SMALL ORANGE
1 TABLESPOON HONEY
SALT

1 Cut the orange slices into 4 and place in a bowl together with the remaining ingredients.

2 Whisk the vinaigrette ingredients together with salt to taste. Pour this into the salad and toss to coat everything in it.

3 Serve lightly chilled.

Moroccan Orange, Carrot, Olive and Chicory Salad

Desserts

LEMON GRANITA

SERVES *6*

PREPARATION *10 minutes*

COOKING *5-6 minutes*

FREEZING *6 hours, plus 30 minutes' ripening*

Calories per serving *104*
Total fat *Low*
Saturated fat *Low*
Protein *Low*
Carbohydrate *High*
Cholesterol *Nil*
Vitamins *C*
Minerals *Potassium*

These Roman water ices are at their best when made with very fresh fruit. Full of flavour, this is the simplest and most refreshing of desserts and is wonderfully cleansing.

4 UNCOATED LEMONS, RINSED
150 G / 5 OZ CASTER SUGAR

6 YOUNG MINT LEAVES, FINELY CHOPPED

1 Grate the rind of 2 of the lemons and set this aside. Squeeze the juice from all of them.
2 Put 600 ml / 1 pint of water in a pan with the sugar and lemon rind. Bring to the boil and simmer for 5-6 minutes. Off the heat, add the mint and lemon juice. Let cool.
3 Empty the mixture into a suitable freezing tray and freeze for at least 6 hours. Take the tray out 2-3 times, at 2-hour intervals, to break the freezing contents up, mixing with a fork or turning it into a bowl and using an electric mixer. It should not freeze into a solid piece, but should have smaller particles.
4 Half an hour before it is to be served, transfer the granita to the refrigerator to allow it to ripen, i.e. make it softer and more pliable – as well as more flavourful. Use a fork again to break up the ice if necessary, before serving.

PEACH GRANITA

There is no more sumptuous finish to a meal on a hot summer evening, or indeed no better treat on a hot summer afternoon. Sometimes I also mix in 3-4 peeled fresh figs for a really exotic effect.

SERVES *6-8*

PREPARATION *20 minutes*

FREEZING *6 hours, plus 15 minutes' ripening*

Calories per serving *73*
Total fat *Low*
Saturated fat *Low*
Protein *Low*
Carbohydrate *High*
Cholesterol *Nil*
Vitamins *C*
Minerals *Potassium*

900 G / 2 LB RIPE PEACHES, PEELED AND STONED
2 TABLESPOONS CASTER SUGAR OR HONEY
2 TABLESPOONS LEMON JUICE
3-4 FRESH FIGS, PEELED AND CHOPPED (OPTIONAL)

TEASPOON VANILLA EXTRACT
2 TABLESPOONS ROSE WATER
6-8 SMALL MINT LEAVES, TO DECORATE

1 If the peaches are ripe they are easy to peel, but if they are hard they have to be blanched quickly in a bowl of boiling water. Stone and slice each one into about 6 pieces.
2 Make a light syrup by boiling the sugar or honey in 150 ml / pint water for 3-4 minutes and then allow this to cool.
3 Place everything in a liquidizer or food processor and purée until smooth.
4 Pour the mixture into a container suitable for a freezer, cover and freeze for 6 hours, taking it out every 2 hours to process again in the food processor or whisk in order to achieve a crystal-free texture.
5 Remove from the freezer about 15 minutes before it is to be served, otherwise it will be too solid. Serve in frozen glasses or bowls and decorate each with a couple of mint leaves.

Lemon Granita

BELILA
An Egyptian Breakfast

Belila is an old Egyptian dessert which has recently become fashionable in smart Cairo hotels, but it has changed its identity and it is now served as a healthy breakfast to the trend- and health-conscious. The dish consists of whole wheat grains which have been boiled and are then served with sweetened milk, nuts and flavourings such as orange flower water or rose water. The wheat expands in volume and should not be overcooked or it will turn into a mass. So keep an eye on it towards the end.

Many variations of the dish can be found round the Mediterranean. For instance, the Greek kolyva *offered at funerals and on All Souls Day is similar but in a dry form without the milk and with a larger variety of nuts and spices. The same can be said about the Turkish* asure, *which has an enormous variety of ingredients – forty according to tradition – and it includes rice and pulses, such as beans and chickpeas, as well as assorted dried fruits. This again is a kind of thick milky pudding and is supposed to be what Noah cooked with all the ingredients he had on the Ark. All these dishes seem related to the ancient Greek* panspermia, *a selection of wheat and nuts offered to the dead and the God of Hades.*

SERVES 6

PREPARATION 10 minutes, plus overnight soaking

COOKING about 1 hour

Calories per serving 380
Total fat *High*
Saturated fat *Low*
Protein *Low*
Carbohydrate *Low*
Cholesterol 10 mg
Vitamins B₁, B₃, B₁₂
Minerals *Iron, Zinc, Iodine*

225 G / 8 OZ WHOLE WHEAT GRAINS, SOAKED OVERNIGHT IN WATER
PINCH OF SALT
425 ML / ¾ PINT MILK
1 TABLESPOON CASTER SUGAR

2 TABLESPOONS AROMATIC HONEY
4 TABLESPOONS ROSE WATER
115 G / 4 OZ FLAKED ALMONDS
50 G / 2 OZ PINE NUTS
SEEDS OF 1 POMEGRANATE (OPTIONAL)

1 Rinse the wheat, place in a pan, cover with water, add salt and bring to the boil. Simmer gently, half-covered, for 35 minutes. Drain.
2 Bring the milk, sugar and honey to the boil, add the wheat and simmer for about 10-15 minutes. Withdraw from the heat and mix in the rose water, nuts and pomegranate seeds.
3 Offer with extra nuts, hot milk and sugar.

TARTA DE NARANJA
Orange Custard

Oranges are the quintessential Mediterranean fruit. Equally, this Spanish dessert instantly evokes the Mediterranean in all its glory. Soft and delectable, it literally melts in the mouth.

SERVES 6

PREPARATION 15-20 minutes

COOKING 45-50 minutes

115 G / 4 OZ CASTER SUGAR OR 3 TABLESPOONS OF AROMATIC HONEY
300 ML / ½ PINT FRESH ORANGE JUICE (4-5 ORANGES), PIPS REMOVED BUT UNSTRAINED

4 EGG YOLKS, PLUS 1 WHOLE EGG
2 TABLESPOONS GROUND ALMONDS
3 TABLESPOONS ROSE WATER
2 TABLESPOONS COARSELY CHOPPED PISTACHIO NUTS

1 Preheat the oven to 160°C/325°F/gas 3.

2 Mix the sugar or honey with 150 ml / ¼ pint water in a pan and boil gently for 4-5 minutes. Add the orange juice and simmer for about 2 minutes until slightly thickened. Let it cool for 10 minutes.

3 In the meantime, beat the eggs in a large bowl until pale and creamy and slowly add the hot orange mixture, beating continuously until smooth. Add the ground almonds and blend them well in. Finally, stir in the rose water and pour the mixture into a small soufflé dish or 6 individual ramekin dishes.

4 Bake in a bain-marie – placing the dish(es) in a larger dish with hot water which comes about halfway up the smaller dish(es) – for about 30-40 minutes until set.

5 Serve warm or lightly chilled. Sprinkle the custard with the pistachio nuts immediately before serving.

Calories per serving *180*
Total fat *High*
Saturated fat *Low*
Protein *Low*
Carbohydrate *Low*
Cholesterol *173 mg*
Vitamins *A, B6, B12, Folate*
Minerals *Calcium, Zinc, Iodine, Potassium*

HOSAF
Turkish Dried Fruit Dessert

Hosaf *is an autumnal dessert common in Turkish homes. Dried fruit of high quality is therefore found in abundance in Turkish markets. A* hosaf *would normally be made up of a selection of fruits, including prunes. One can improvise, and alter the varieties of fruit suggested below according to availability. The addition of different nuts, like the pine nuts, makes the dish more luxurious and the final sprinkling of scarlet pomegranate seeds adds an extra layer of flavour as well as a fairy-tale hint of the East.*

175 G / 6 OZ PRUNES
175 G / 6 OZ DRIED FIGS
115 G / 4 OZ DRIED APRICOTS
50 G / 2 OZ RAISINS
2 TABLESPOONS WHOLE SHELLED ALMONDS
1 TABLESPOON SUGAR

1 TABLESPOON HONEY
3 TABLESPOONS ROSE WATER

FOR DECORATION:
SEEDS OF 1 POMEGRANATE (SEE PAGE 19)
1 TABLESPOON PINE NUTS, TOASTED

SERVES 6

PREPARATION *5-10 minutes*

COOKING *about 20 minutes, plus 4 hours' standing*

Calories per serving *221*
Total fat *Low*
Saturated fat *Low*
Protein *Low*
Carbohydrate *High*
Cholesterol *Nil*
Vitamins *B2, B6, E*
Minerals *Calcium, Potassium, Iron, Zinc*

1 Several hours ahead of serving, or ideally the day before: rinse and drain the dried fruit. Boil the shelled almonds for 2-3 minutes, drain them and when they are cool enough to handle, skin them.

2 Mix the sugar and honey with 900 ml / 1½ pints of water in a stainless steel pan and bring to the boil. Add the fruit and simmer for 15 minutes. Add the almonds and simmer for 5 minutes more.

3 Stir in the rose water and leave the fruit to macerate in the syrup for at least 4 hours or preferably overnight.

4 Serve at room temperature or warm up slightly. Scatter the pomegranate seeds and the pine nuts all over just before serving.

BAKED PEACHES WITH PISTACHIO NUTS

6 RIPE BUT FIRM PEACHES, HALVED AND STONED

175 G / 6 OZ SHELLED PISTACHIOS

2 MACAROONS OR AMARETTI BISCUITS

2 TABLESPOONS GROUND ALMONDS

2 TABLESPOONS CASTER SUGAR

½ TEASPOON GROUND CINNAMON

1 EGG YOLK

3 TABLESPOONS ORANGE BLOSSOM OR ROSE WATER

LIGHT FROMAGE FRAIS OR PLAIN LOW-FAT YOGHURT, TO SERVE (OPTIONAL)

FOR THE SYRUP:

2-3 TABLESPOONS HONEY

2 CINNAMON STICKS

FEW STRIPS OF ORANGE PEEL

2 TABLESPOONS ORANGE BLOSSOM OR ROSE WATER

1 Preheat the oven to 180°C/350°F/gas 4.

2 Coarsely chop the pistachio nuts and biscuits (this is quicker in a food processor). Empty into a bowl and mix into a paste with the almonds, sugar, cinnamon, egg yolk and orange blossom water or rose water.

3 Fill the cavity of each peach generously with this mixture, and arrange the fruit closely in a medium-sized baking dish.

4 Make the syrup: dissolve the honey in 300 ml / ½ pint of water over gentle heat, add the cinnamon and peel and boil for 5-6 minutes until slightly thickened. Add the orange or rose water and pour around the peaches.

5 Bake for 15 minutes, until the peaches look soft without falling apart, basting occasionally. The peaches are delicious on their own, or serve them with fromage frais or yoghurt.

SERVES 6

PREPARATION *about 20 minutes*

COOKING *about 20 minutes*

Calories per serving *218*
Total fat *High*
Saturated fat *Low*
Protein *Low*
Carbohydrate *Low*
Cholesterol *34 mg*
Vitamins B_1, B_3, B_{12}, C, E
Minerals *Calcium, Potassium, Iron, Zinc, Iodine,*

FIGS WITH MARSALA AND ORANGE

8-12 FIRM FRESH FIGS

150 ML / ¼ PINT MARSALA OR A SWEET MUSCAT WINE SUCH AS SAMOS

JUICE OF 2 ORANGES PLUS THE ZEST OF ONE, SLICED INTO THIN JULIENNE STRIPS

2 TABLESPOONS AROMATIC HONEY

4 TABLESPOONS ORANGE FLOWER WATER OR ROSE WATER, OR 1 TEASPOON VANILLA EXTRACT

2 TABLESPOONS CRÈME FRAÎCHE (OPTIONAL)

8 YOUNG MINT LEAVES (OPTIONAL)

1 Combine the orange juice and Marsala or wine in a stainless steel saucepan. Bring to the boil and boil rapidly for 5 minutes to reduce it. Mix in the honey and the orange zest and simmer for 3-4 more minutes.

2 Place the figs in the pan and roll them around in the syrup over a gentle heat to poach them for 2 minutes. They should not cook and soften but remain intact.

3 Off the heat, add the orange flower water, rose water or vanilla and let it cool. Chill in the refrigerator for at least 1 hour.

4 Serve slightly chilled, coating the figs with their syrup.

SERVES 4

PREPARATION *10 minutes*

COOKING *about 10 minutes, plus cooling and chilling*

Calories per serving *162*
Total fat *Medium*
Saturated fat *Medium*
Protein *Low*
Carbohydrate *Medium*
Cholesterol *10 mg*
Vitamins *C*
Minerals *Iron, Potassium*

Baked Peaches with Pistachio Nuts

PLUM OR PEACH CLAFOUTIS

This is one of the easiest, lightest and most versatile desserts to prepare. When we are at home on the Greek island of Alonnisos, as the summer proceeds I make it using different kinds of fruit.

In early July it is the small, bright yellow and honeyed local apricots. Our old friend Barba Nikos, who owns orchards of apricot trees, arrives early in the morning with quantities of aromatic fruit. Then the race is on to use them all. They make the most sumptuous jam; stewed apricots with Greek yoghurt are served after lunch, and in the evenings the aroma of the freshly baked clafoutis spilling into the garden is irresistible.

Then the huge rosy-skinned peaches appear, to be followed by the juicy purple plums. Occasionally we pick small but very sweet blackberries from the hedges in the hillsides, and these are scattered over the other fruit in the clafoutis.

By the end of August, when our grapes start to ripen, I include a small bunch of these for good measure. The grapes have to be split in half and deseeded before they join the rest of the fruit.

Originally, of course, clafoutis was traditionally made with cherries and served during the cherry-picking season in the Limousin region of France.

SERVES 4-6

PREPARATION
20 minutes

COOKING
about 50 minutes

Calories per serving *229*
Total fat *Medium*
Saturated fat *Medium*
Protein *Low*
Carbohydrate *Medium*
Cholesterol *150 mg*
Vitamins *A, B₂, B₃, B₆, B₁₂,*
Folate, C
Minerals *Calcium,*
Potassium, Iron, Iodine

550 G / 1 LB 4 OZ PURPLE PLUMS, OR PEACHES
½ TEASPOON SOFTENED BUTTER, FOR THE DISH
2 TABLESPOONS CASTER SUGAR

FOR THE BATTER:
3 EGGS

50 G / 2 OZ CASTER SUGAR
300 ML / ½ PINT MILK
50 G / 2 OZ PLAIN FLOUR, SIFTED WITH A PINCH OF SALT
1 TABLESPOON PURE VANILLA EXTRACT
LARGE PINCH OF GROUND CINNAMON

1 Preheat the oven to 190°C/375°F/gas 5 and butter a 25 cm / 10 in flan dish or similar baking dish.
2 Slice the plums in half and stone them. If using peaches, first blanch them briefly in boiling water. Then skin and stone them, and cut them into quarters.
3 Arrange the fruit in the dish, skin down and in one layer closely packed. Sprinkle the sugar all over the top.

4 Make the batter: mix the eggs, sugar and milk together in the blender, add the flour, vanilla and cinnamon and blend until smooth.
5 Pour the batter mixture over the fruit and bake for about 50 minutes, until quite risen and golden on top. It will be studded with the colourful fruit, and the juices of the fruit will have made the dish meltingly soft and sweet.
6 Clafoutis is best served hot or warm.

Plum Clafoutis

INDEX

ACKNOWLEDGMENTS

Godmother to the idea of this book was Jo Christian. She was determined to get the project off the ground and it has been a real pleasure for me to work with her as she has been supportive and inspirational throughout.

The good looks of the book are due to the enthusiasm and commitment of Louise Tucker. I am also grateful to a number of other people at Frances Lincoln for their support, particularly to Anne Fraser and Sue Gladstone.

However, the person to whom I am most grateful is Lewis Esson. He has been a wonderful and very patient editor who has always shown great sensitivity in managing an extra-long manuscript.

I feel privileged to have Gus Filgate's beautiful photographs in the book, as these brilliantly convey the very soul of the Mediterranean. I am also grateful to Louise Pickford for cooking and presenting the dishes so artfully.

Also thanks to my agent Caroline Davidson for arranging everything.

I am, of course, indebted to all my friends who have generously given recipes and advice. In particular Cecile Harris, Vera Kyriakou, Sami Zubaida, Gillian Riley, Henrietta Valvini and Anna Del Conte. Also my thanks to Ursula Arens at the British Nutrition Foundation, for answering all my queries so promptly; and to my sister, Sally Printzios and all our friends on the island of Alonnisos, particularly Barba Nikos (who, unfortunately, will not be able to read this). My appreciation also goes to classicist Andrew Dalby for his wonderful book *Siren Feasts*, from which I have learned so much, and whose translations of Homer I have quoted here and there.

Lastly my thanks go to my daughters, who tried almost everything and offered very explicit criticism; and to Graeme for his support, his large appetite and his critical palate.

Editor & Project Manager: Lewis Esson
Designer: Siân Keogh
Photography: Gus Filgate
Styling: Penny Markham
Food Styling: Louise Pickford
Research: Sue Gladstone
Editorial Assistance: Penny David
Nutritional Analysis: Patricia Bacon
Indexer: Hilary Bird
Production: Jennifer Cohen
Design Styling: Sally Cracknell
Art Editor: Louise Tucker
Picture Editor: Anne Fraser
Editorial Director: Erica Hunningher
Art Director: Caroline Hillier